147 Practical Tips for Teaching Peace and Reconciliation

by
William M. Timpson, Edward J. Brantmeier,
Nathalie Kees, Tom Cavanagh, Claire McGlynn,
and Elavie Ndura-Ouédraogo

Atwood Publishing
Madison, WI

147 Practical Tips for Teaching Peace and Reconciliation
By William M. Timpson, Edward J. Brantmeier, Nathalie Kees, Tom Cavanagh, Claire
McGlynn, and Elavie Ndura-Ouédraogo
ISBN: 978-1-891859-76-2
© 2009 Atwood Publishing, Madison, WI
www.atwoodpublishing.com

Cover design by Tamara Dever, TLC Graphics, www.tlcgraphics.com

Library of Congress Cataloging-in-Publication Data

147 tips for teaching peace and reconciliation / William M. Timpson ...[et al.].
    p. cm.
  Includes bibliographical references and index.
  ISBN 978-1-891859-76-2 (pbk. : alk. paper) 1. Peace—Study and teaching. 2.
Reconciliation—Study and teaching. 3. Conflict management—Study and teaching. I.
Timpson, William M. II. Title: One hundred forty-seven tips for teaching peace and
reconciliation. III. Title: One hundred and forty-seven tips for teaching peace and
reconciliation.
  JZ5534.A23 2010
  303.6'6071—dc22
                          2009028117

Dedications

To peacemakers of all ages and in all places,
To those who challenge us to go deeper, broader, and higher,
And to Maury Albertson, colleague and friend, a visionary and tireless advocate
for sustainable development who helped birth the Peace Corps
—William M. Timpson

To my son, Ian William, who was born during this book project,
may you continue to learn and love the ways of peace.
—Edward J. Brantmeier

To all those who peacefully walk this earth.
—Nathalie Kees

In memory of Te Whiti o Rongomai and Tohu Kakahi,
Maori prophets of peace and non-violence.
—Tom Cavanagh

To my nephew, John Knight, who was also born during this project,
may you experience peace.
—Claire McGlynn

To all who have been victimized by human conflict, violence, and war,
may we find in our pain the love and strength to live for peace.
—Elavie Ndura-Ouédraogo

Acknowledgments

To Kathryn A. Wright for copy editing
To Kellee Timpson for editing assistance

To all the Contributors:

Antonette Aragon	James Banning
Lisa Barrett	Mallorie Bruns
James Clausen	Wendy Cohen
Ellyn Dickmann	Viviane Ephraimson-Abt
James Folkestad	Jen Fullerton
Maggie Graham	Debra Kaye Holman
Saun Hutchins	Stefanie Kendall
Gailmarie Kimmel	Stephanie King
Katy Kirk	Meredith Laine
Sonja Modesti	Stephanie Moyers
Dean Nelson	Cassandra Poncelow
Daniel Reinholz	Rich Salas
Guadalupe Salazar	Andrea Taylor
Kellee Timpson	Ana Tomovska
Kim Watchorn	Jayme Winell

TABLE OF CONTENTS

PREFACE
Coming Together to Create

William M. Timpson

The idea for this book arose from several sources. First, there is the continuing toll of warfare and violence throughout the world. For me, it was the Iraq War, in particular, with all its tragic, wasteful, and costly consequences. The questions that continue to haunt me are many: How did this war, in particular, happen, especially when there was so much public opposition worldwide? How could we, the citizens of the United States, in particular, have let it happen? How do any of us balance our responsibilities to support our fellow citizens in uniform, to attend to the needs of returning veterans—and especially the wounded, scarred, and traumatized—with the importance of critical analysis and democratic dissent, of challenging the decisions that led to violence? And how do we reconcile the bitter legacy of differences that is heightened by war and then polarizes the political process for years to come?

Yet, I was simultaneously inspired by examples of successful and recent efforts at peacemaking around the world, where bitter and longstanding hatreds were being challenged and transformed with new policies and practices. As the incoming Program Chair for the Special Interest Group (SIG) in Peace Education at the 2008 annual meeting of the American Educational Research Association (AERA), I found much hope in the detailed reports about educators who were taking the lead in working toward peace and reconciliation in very troubled areas, in Northern Ireland and the Middle East, in the post-genocide Great Lakes Region of central Africa, as well as post-apartheid South Africa.

Given these very mixed feelings, I felt a strong sense of urgency to continue studying the negatives while building on the positives. While many of us worked in relative isolation from each other, I knew that we could benefit from the synergy of a collaborative project where we could support and assist each other, pool our expertise and learn from each other, identify what worked, and, hopefully, generate some new insights as well.

I knew that a new collaborative project on peace and reconciliation was very possible. In 2005 I had gathered several colleagues around me to draw on our earlier book, *Teaching Diversity,* to write *147 Practical Tips for Teaching Diversity,* a volume of practical and concise instructional ideas, for a series with Atwood Publishing. Soon thereafter I drew together another team to write *147 Practical Tips for Teaching Sustainability* (2006). I was becoming increasingly committed to the idea that educators could—and should—apply their understanding of instruction and learning to the compelling issues of the day, helping students and instructors, as well as those in the larger community, tap into a bank of ideas and proven practices to address difficult, complex, and sensitive problems.

Fortunately, I had a wonderful and longstanding relationship with Linda Babler at Atwood Publishing. Similarly outraged by the ideological extremism of the George W. Bush administration and its reckless use of the U.S. military for its foreign ambitions, Linda gave her wholehearted support to the idea of a new book on teaching peace and reconciliation. Even though other publishers were scared of book projects with "peace" in their titles, Babler was quick to commit the resources of Atwood Publishing to supporting our proposed project.

With that commitment in hand, I felt encouraged to approach other scholars active in peace education. Claire McGlynn from Queen's University in Belfast, Northern Ireland, was quick to agree. She has been doing such important work with the integrated schools movement, in particular, researching new approaches to integration that help students unlearn longstanding hatreds and cross their deeply divided society, developing the skills needed to communicate with and appreciate those who are different.

My colleague Tom Cavanagh also agreed, bringing a wealth of experience and groundbreaking work on restorative practices and the culture of care. Tom had spent many years working as a court reporter in the U.S. and became increasingly upset by the "revolving door" of those convicted, jailed, released and returned, people who all too often were poor or marginalized by their differences of ethnic origin. Tom came to Colorado State University to work on his Ph.D. in education and human resource studies, and specifically in restorative practices for schools and communities. Once graduated, Tom was awarded a Fulbright to continue his research in New Zealand, where many of the ideas for restorative practices originated. While in New Zealand he was privileged to learn how Maori (the indigenous people of New Zealand) traditionally responded to wrongdoing and conflict.

At our annual meetings for AERA's Peace Education SIG, I was fortunate to hear about the work on reconciliation of Elavie Ndura-Ouédraogo, a Native-born scholar from Burundi who had fled the genocide around her country, emigrated to the U.S., and was now on the faculty at George Mason University. Despite losing her husband, Elavie has continued to return to her native lands to help rebuild the schools, refashion the curriculum, heal the deep wounds, and point toward an inclusive, peaceful way forward.

Finally, I also recruited two colleagues from my own campus, knowing how much I personally benefitted from the support of others close by, from the synergy that was possible when I could share ideas with colleagues, observe them teach, and we could all learn from each other. Ed Brantmeier had recently joined our faculty in the School of Education at Colorado State University, bringing much international experience along with expertise and commitment to both multicultural and peace education. Ed is a prolific scholar who had recently published his own edited book of case studies on peace education while beginning work as co-editor on an entirely new series of books on peace education as well.

Also on our faculty at Colorado State is Nathalie Kees, a counselor by training, who had taught me much about the mindfulness work of Thich Nhat Hanh, the Buddhist Vietnamese monk and author who has led peacemaking seminars all over the world. Nathalie has developed a new course on contemplative practices for counselors at Colorado State University that integrates the wisdom of various spiritual traditions. She has also joined the Board for our University's Interdisciplinary Program in Peace and Reconciliation Studies that offers undergraduates and graduates a structured program of coursework and other credited experiences.

My own background blends well with those I recruited for this project. Growing up in the Roxbury section of Boston and then teaching in the inner city of Cleveland, I was immersed in the daily issues of predominantly African American communities and their struggles with historic racism, violence, and limited opportunities. As a recipient of a Kellogg National Fellowship Award, I was later able to broaden my experiences with extensive travels overseas, exploring cultures, oppression, violence, and education in Cuba, Nicaragua, Brazil, China, and Europe. Selected as a Fulbright Senior Specialist for Peace and Reconciliation Studies in 2005, I have also completed two extended stays in Northern Ireland which have helped immeasurably with my work on this book.

So come join this exciting, complex, and compelling study of teaching for peace and reconciliation. While our "147 Tips" only touch the surface of this work, we do offer many references that point to the writings of great peacemakers and dedicated scholars. And let this be a beginning. Explore the ideas we offer, and then make the necessary adaptations for your own setting. Add your own ideas. Together we can deepen and broaden our current thinking about peace and reconciliation. With studied practice, we can help lessen the scourge of violence and militarism everywhere.

INTRODUCTION

Edward Brantmeier, William M. Timpson,
Nathalie Kees, Tom Cavanagh, Claire McGlynn,
and Elavie Ndura-Ouédraogo

For many of us, abstractions, concepts, and theories can be quite removed from the realities of everyday issues, especially when teaching and learning peace and reconciliation. Yet, theory—a realm of concepts, ideas, and principles—is essential for responding to the larger questions, trends, and patterns we find in life. Often, what we need are practical bridges between theory and the day-to-day realities of people in our increasingly interdependent world. These bridges can help generate new insights and make us more aware of our efforts toward building peace and justice in a world too often violent and dangerous. This book attempts to build these bridges between theory and the everyday world of educators in schools as well as leaders in various community organizations, businesses, and other social institutions who grapple with the complexities of peace, justice, reconciliation, conflict, diversity, unity, and sustainability. It does so by providing practical tips for teaching peace and reconciliation that are rooted in a variety of theoretical and practical orientations.

A strong interdisciplinary approach is essential in order to expand the horizons of peace education for theoreticians and practitioners alike (Bekerman and McGlynn 2007). An interdisciplinary and global initiative at heart, this collaborative effort brought together scholars, students, and educators, both seasoned and emergent, to draw on their experiences and creativity and to engage in a practical dialogue with the available literature on peace and reconciliation studies. In particular, we asked members of the Peace Education Special Interest Groups of the American Educational Research Association and the Comparative and International Education Society to contribute their ideas. We wanted to blend some of the established theories and practices in the field with new, different and innovative ideas. We also asked our own students to contribute their ideas and experiences in learning about peace and reconciliation. We thank all contributors for sharing their experiences and ideas; this diversity, directed toward common goals, is both inspiring and renewing. As such, we recognize the value of paying close attention to the personal and professional knowledge of peace educators (Bekerman and McGlynn 2007). Our diversity multiplies the strength of us all—a real synergy indeed.

Our hope is that different people will use these concise and practical tips as springboards for promoting peace and reconciliation in schools, colleges and universities, other organizations, in communities and other groups, locally and around the world. We do not assume that these tips will be universally accepted and usable; it will often be necessary to make adaptations for particular environments. Recognition that education is bound by socio-historical-political conditions is a crucial step towards developing context-sensitive approaches to peace education (McGlynn, Zembylas, Bekerman, and Gallagher 2009). Rarely are there simple blueprints or easy solutions to remedy, alleviate, or transform the violence in our hearts, minds, homes, communities, societies, and world. However, if we are to live sustainably in the future, *we must work to actualize the ideals of peace and reconciliation*. Drawing on previous manuscripts that described similar concrete and practical ideas ("Tips") for teaching diversity and sustainability, my colleagues and I provide a template for this kind of transdisciplinary work (Timpson et al. 2005; Timpson et al. 2006).

Doing Peace and Reconciliation

Ian Harris and John Synott (2002) provide a broad definition of peace education as "teaching encounters that draw out from people their desires for peace and provide them with nonviolent alternatives for managing conflicts, as well as the skills for critical analysis of the structural arrangements that legitimate and produce *injustice* and *inequality*" (4). Several assumptions are at work here. First, desires for peace cannot be imposed on people using an authoritative "teacher knows all" approach. Banking models of education, where teachers are depositors of knowledge and students are receptacles of that knowledge (Freire 1970), cannot work either, because the means and the ends of peace education are not aligned. Instead, ideas and plans for peace should be *drawn out* from people using a pedagogy that models peaceful processes and assures the dignity, respect, and rights of every learner. In fact, educators become co-learners in the process of meaning-making and mutual discovery. In *Teaching and Learning Peace,* Bill Timpson (2002) describes the mechanisms for using inquiry and other inductive approaches to deepen learning and expand critical and creative thinking.

However, peaceful approaches to the learning process are only one important factor. According to Harris and Synott (2002), peace education also needs to provide specific skills for managing conflicts effectively and nonviolently. Contributors to this book offer a range of practical tips about human relations skills, including how to communicate effectively, listen deeply and reflectively, take perspective, reserve judgment, demonstrate acceptance and build empathy, mediate, negotiate and manage conflicts, and build consensus. Without these, peace and reconciliation often remain lofty abstractions far removed from our realistic capabilities. Contributors to this book draw from various disciplines to offer practical approaches to building the skills necessary for managing and transforming conflicts that are often inherently complex and exist on many levels (i.e., environmental, intrapersonal, interpersonal, intergroup, societal, national, and international).

In addition to learning conflict resolution skills, Tom Cavanagh (2007) suggests that a culture of care in organizations needs to be created wherein people learn how to respond nonviolently to wrongdoing and conflict. This responsive caring capacity can actually be embedded and engender greater consistency. Nel Noddings' (1992) emphasizes that this ethic of care can be extended to the whole organization so that creating and maintaining healthy, positive relationships becomes a core responsibility of everyone. A cultural shift is often required because the prevailing response to conflict is all too often ineffective, either ignoring it, eliminating it, or sending it away for an expert to solve. Within a culture of care, conflict emerges as a potentially positive personal and communal opportunity to affirm caring relationships while navigating differences.

When asked to identify major themes that comprise the heart of this book, the lead authors agreed that the way we think about peace impacts what we do and how we teach. This is an important point to consider given that our understanding of conflict, challenges, contexts, and/or problems can enable or constrain our creative abilities to manage, resolve, or transform them. Being conscious of how our thinking impacts the outcomes of the peace and reconciliation processes and being flexible, fluid, and willing to change our perspectives, approaches, and paradigms are vital for actualizing peace and reconciliation.

Linda Groff (2002) provides a typology for thinking about peace that might aid our understanding of possible levels of peace. Because Groff positions peace thinking on global, international, national, societal, communal, inter-group, environmental, interpersonal, and intrapersonal levels, an understanding of the interdependence of these levels is vital for movement from a mechanistic, fractionalized worldview toward an inclusive, fluid, and interdependent worldview. Peace thinking and transformative action become complex and powerful when individuals and groups become conscious of the interdependent dimensions of their efforts. It assures us that what we do matters and has positive impact elsewhere. Several tips in this book attempt to promote this conscious, engaged action toward actualizing a nonviolent, sustainable future.

Toward a Paradigm of Peace, Reconciliation, and Hope

Moving away from violence as a means of resolving conflicts and toward a commitment to reconciliation requires compassion, forgiveness, and a desire for a more sustainable future. Moving away from a nationalistic and militaristic paradigm toward a humanistic and diplomatic paradigm requires a wider global identification, a morally inclusive orientation, and a desire for constructive and creative means to peaceful ends. Moving from a defensive to an inclusive stance on security requires a shift from self-interest to other-centeredness that embraces all people and the planet as an interdependent community. Moving away from a false harmony and toward a diversity affirming paradigm requires critical analysis of the structural violence that favors some at the expense of others; it requires a critical examination of power, privilege, marginalization, and the dynamics of difference that often reproduce social stratification and inequality (Brantmeier and Lin 2008). We wholeheartedly agree with Ian Harris and John Synott (2002), who maintain that peace education must provide the tools to directly challenge injustice and inequality.

A further unanimous theme among the authors of this book is acknowledging the close link between peace education discourse and human diversity discourse. Several of the tips provided in this book assume that we cannot effectively teach peace while avoiding raising difficult questions about human diversity. In *Teaching Diversity*, Bill Timpson, Silvia Canetto, Ray Yang, and Evelinn Borrayo (2003) note how addressing issues of ethnicity, social class, gender, privilege, power and powerlessness in the classroom can evoke feelings of resistance and rage. The attainment of an authentic peace will be difficult, if not impossible, without the dialogue, practice, and policies that affirm human diversity and establish common ground (Kees 2003). However, cultural assimilation and coerced conformity can also be forms of violence that must be questioned. So how do we promote, embrace, sustain, and honor multiple layers of our identities amid pressures to conform to the powers that be? How do we transform these powers into peaceful forces?

The authors agree that a peace pedagogy, effective communication and pro-social skills, new thinking about conflicts including critical analysis, reconciliation, and engaged constructive action—within a culture that supports building and maintaining peaceful and caring relationships—are all needed for actualizing peace and a sustainable future. In addition, teaching peace needs to be connected to core values such as honesty, integrity, equality, and equity. Ed Brantmeier and Jing Lin (2008) go even further and insist that "peace education efforts need to be linked to social justice. Examining power, oppression, privilege, and social stratification in relation to gender, class, race, dis/ability, sexual orientation, religion, national origin, and language are essential" (xv). Elavie Ndura (2007) then claims that conscious and engaged citizens will also reject politically correct discourses that promote individual and structural hypocrisy, and consciously invest their talents, time, and resources in the eradication of racism, classism, sexism, and other forms of oppressive injustice. These citizens labor to build diverse communities devoid of fear, tension, and suspicion. All of these ideas and commitments undergird the "tips" provided in this book.

Lastly, but surely no less importantly, the authors have come to believe that cultivating inner peace also emerges as a necessity to actualizing nonviolent futures. Inner peace is connected to outer peace in a mutually inclusive manner. In this light, many "tips" in this book assume that the cultivation of inner peace is of the utmost importance in order to actualize relational peace. The self, society, and the planet comprise different, yet interdependent domains for working on peace and reconciliation. In healing ourselves, we can heal our societies. In healing our societies, we can heal ourselves. In healing ourselves and our societies, we can heal this beautiful planet we depend upon. In building a culture of peace and justice, we can renew our hope and aspirations to leave the children of the world a sustainable future. We offer you, the readers, the gifts of life and hope in our efforts toward peace and reconciliation.

UNDERSTANDING PEACE EDUCATION

We need a blending of the old and the new, the proven and the possible, in the field of peace education. We need to understand what scholars, activists, and leaders have said about peace education. However, we also need to hear from those who are developing new ideas and forging connections with curricula in other disciplines. Accordingly, we call for the integration of theory, research, practice, and vision. In order to bridge the historic fault lines of conflict and violence with contemporary concerns of injustice and inequality, we must challenge privilege, counter oppression, appreciate diversity, and promote inclusiveness. Finally, we must develop transformative leadership at every level of society.

1. Rethink the War and Dominance Paradigms

The telling of history from limited, violence-based perspectives constructs social memory in ways that help to perpetuate violence as inherent, natural, and a human absolute—in short, 'just the way things are.' The telling of violent histories saturates collective memory with violent images and struggles of the past; these violent narratives can serve to impact the power of present transformative action toward actualizing nonviolent futures. In *Cultures of Peace: The Hidden Side of History*, Elise Boulding (2000) writes of the war-steeped telling of history as related to western civilization, that history is often written as stories about the rise and fall of empires, a description of the rulers, their armies, navies and air power, their wars and battles, i.e., the history of power—who controls whom.

In this provocative book, Boulding critiques the telling of history from violent, power-dominated, and patriarchal viewpoints. She furthers her argument by providing historical examples of groups and societies who lived relatively peaceful and harmonious lives, solving conflict in nonviolent ways.

Examine how you and participants are/were "told" stories in history books and various media. What explicit and implicit messages are reinforced through these narratives? Brainstorm a list of examples of nonviolent historic responses to conflict situations. Who were the key players, leaders, and 'behind the scenes' people and groups involved in these conflicts? What methods, besides violence, were used to actualize change? Reflect on how peaceful, nonviolent, and cooperative paradigms might alternatively transform present community, societal, national, and global conflicts into mutually beneficial outcomes for humanity and our fellow planetary inhabitants.

2. Create Concentric Circles for Positive Peace

Johan Galtung (1969, 1988) infused peace theory, or a set of principles that guide peace thinking and peace education practices, with the concepts of negative peace and positive peace. Negative peace can be understood as the absence of direct physical violence—war, domestic violence, etc. Positive peace can be understood as conditions without indirect violence—a lack of trust, intimidation, the presence of fear, bullying, or conditions without structural violence. Educative efforts toward positive peace seek to build new macrostructural alignments that promote capacity, prosperity, and happiness for all, as well as trust in peace, trust in relationships, hope, and reflection on positive conditions that create peace.

The activity provides an opportunity for people to reflect on past, present, and future conditions of peace, thus generating positive memories, present mindfulness, and future possibilities. Outside or in a large room, ask a group to form two circles with even numbers—one inner circle, one outer circle. People should stand face to face. Ask them to introduce themselves to their partner. Use the following series of questions and time each question (about 3 minutes each), and then rotate. "Describe a peaceful time in your life." After 3 minutes of back and forth discussion, ask the inner or outer circle to move one, two, or three people to the left or to the right; this promotes interaction with multiple members of the circle. Then say: "Describe a time when there was peace in your community, your nation, or the world." Then ask them to fill in the blank: "I currently find peace when ____; my community finds peace when____; the nation ____; the world ____." Finally, ask them to fill in the blanks: "I will find peace when_____; my community will find peace when _____; the nation____; the world____." Debrief by identifying the conditions for peace from the personal to the global level; write them on a chart.

3. Enhance Holistic Peace Thinking

Linda Groff (2002) positions the need for "peace thinking" on multiple, interdependent levels in order to actualize a peaceful world. This model includes Galtung's (1969, 1988) distinction of negative and positive peace. It also adds the level of integrated peace—holistic and systemic conceptions of what peace could look like among cultural groups, between the human and non-human world, and peace that holistically integrates outer forms of peace and inner forms of peace. The benefit of using Groff's conceptual model for thinking about peace is that it adds the more complex "integrated peace" dimension and it includes vital foci on feminist, intercultural, planetary, and inner peace.

Groff's model (2002) delineates seven central concepts in peace thinking:

1. War Prevention (Negative Peace)
   a. Peace as Absence of War
   b. Peace as Balance of Forces in the International System

2. Structural Conditions for Peace (Positive Peace)
   a. Peace as no war and no structural violence on macro levels
   b. Peace as no war and no structural violence on micro levels (Community, Family, Feminist Peace)

3. Peace Thinking that Stresses Holistic, Complex Systems (Integrated Peace)
   a. Intercultural Peace (peace among cultural groups)
   b. Holistic Gaia Peace (Peace within the human world and with the environment).
   c. Holistic Inner and Outer Peace (Includes all 6 types of peace and adds inner peace as essential condition) (7-8).

Facilitate a group brainstorm about specific actions that would contribute to peace at each level of Groff's model. Guide a conversation about how these various levels of peace thinking are interconnected and also unique. Then have a conversation about how one can work to promote peace on various levels.

4. Create a Violence Tree: Track Everyday Acts of Indirect and Direct Violence

Nonviolent activist Arun Gandhi, grandson of the great Mahatma Gandhi of India, and co-founder with his wife Sunanda of the M. K. Gandhi Institute for Nonviolence, shares personal stories with audiences in the United States and around the world of his childhood growing up under the tutelage of the Mahatma at his ashram in Gujarat, India (Gandhi 2003). One of the stories that he shares is M. K. Gandhi's use of a violence tree, similar to a family tree, to help trace acts of both direct and indirect violence committed by an individual on a daily basis.

Start with the terms direct and indirect violence at the top of their violence trees. Trace all acts of direct violence for the day: e.g., "I stepped on an ant; I killed a mosquito; I punched a friend in the shoulder for saying the wrong thing."

Then trace all acts of indirect violence: e.g., "I wished that somebody would suffer for their pride; I intimidated a co-worker; I felt jealousy for someone else's success." Examine how certain acts of violence lead to others and how different forms of violence are related. Reflect on these acts of direct or indirect violence and how they harm others. Vow to make changes the following day. Record those changes and other acts of violence committed as time moves on.

5. Map Peace and Violence Toward Local Change

Everyday understandings of peace and non-peace can vary from one sociocultural context to another, given the unique realities and dynamics of those contexts. Mapping everyday understandings of peace and violence is a research technique that can be used to determine both conceptions of peace and non-peace; it can be used to identify peaceful and non-peaceful attitudes and behaviors in local contexts. These conceptions and identifications can then be used to engage local, cultural actors in transformative change processes (Brantmeier 2007).

As a warm up, make a list on a sheet of paper of words that "go with peace," and then words that "go with non-peace." Circle the two most important words. Identify peaceful attitudes and behaviors in everyday life (classroom, school, community, church, city, etc…). Now identify non-peaceful attitudes and behaviors. Circle the two most important. If you are leading a group, record the most important responses on a flip chart or chalk board. You can also share stories, either your own or what you've observed, both peaceful and nonpeaceful. Take notes, or record the stories that are shared. Ask some of the following questions: How can peaceful attitudes and behaviors multiply in this context? How can non-peaceful attitudes and behaviors be changed? From this list, create action plans to enhance what is peaceful and change what's not.

6. Conduct a Webbing Exercise: Know that Violence Impacts Us All

Understanding the interdependence of all life through experiencing connection is helpful for living peacefully/nonviolently. M. K. Gandhi wrote, "I believe in non-duality (*advaita*), I believe in the essential unity of man and, for that matter, of all that lives… The rock bottom foundation of the technique for achieving the power of nonviolence is belief in the essential oneness of all life" (Young India, December 4, 1924, in Collected Works, 25: 390). Cultivating an experience of interdependence provides an emotive ground for non-violent action and peaceful relationships among group members.

Ask a few individuals in a group to represent non-human life (wolves, fish, bugs, plants, reptiles etc…). Give them a sign with the name or picture of this animal or plant. Assemble the group into a circle in a large space. Start with a colorful ball of yarn, pick someone, state a positive comment about that person, and pass the ball of yarn to him or her. That person does the same for someone else, until all are connected via the ball of yarn. When everyone is connected, ask the group what this web represents. Have one individual drop the yarn, turn away from the group, or tense or loosen the web. Discuss how this impacts the whole. What if an animal or plant becomes extinct? Ask how an individual act of violence impacts us all; what about an act of kindness? Ask what this web might represent in everyday life.

7. Make Meaningful Contact and Reduce Conflict

In conflict-ridden societies, much investment is often made in educational contact schemes designed to bring young people from the divided groups together in short- and long-term encounters with the aim of reducing prejudice towards the "other" and hopefully thus ameliorating conflict. This approach draws on *contact theory* (Allport 1954), the notion that working together on a common goal will do the most to reduce hostile feelings and build appreciation, and a subsequent litany of conditions for success. In Northern Ireland, for example, contact theory underpins much peace education endeavour, both in the formal and informal education sectors.

After many years of extensive empirical research into the efficacy of inter-group contact in Israel and elsewhere, Gavriel Salomon (2007) concluded that there are two fundamental success criteria. Firstly, there must be a very important common goal for the two groups to work towards together, and secondly, there must be the opportunity for sustainable friendships to emerge from the contact.

Consider the work that you do in bringing together people with little experience of the "other." How might Salomon's main criteria influence the way in which you design educational policy and practice with regards to reducing inter-group prejudice? What kind of common goals would be appropriate in your educational environment and how, as an educator, can you support the development of inter-group friendships? Can you think of further success criteria that could help maximize the success of educational contact experiences in your institution or organization?

8. Understand How Oppression Sparks Violence

In his seminal book *Pedagogy of the Oppressed,* Paulo Freire (1970) argues that dehumanization marks out not only those whose humanity has been stolen, but also those who steal it, that is, the oppressors. To Freire, dehumanization distorts any growth towards becoming more fully human and sooner or later, this loss of humanity leads the oppressed to struggle for humanization, emancipation, and affirmation as persons, and to overcome their feelings of alienation. Only the oppressed can truly liberate both themselves and their oppressors. The latter, who are dehumanized because their oppressing dehumanizes others, do not have the power to transform the situation. However the oppressed must resist, in turn, oppressing their oppressors during the search to regain their humanity.

Consider a number of examples of dehumanization of the "other" in former and recent conflicts around the world and critically analyze to what extent you think that Freire's concept of dehumanization is appropriate. Debate the role that formal and informal education might play in supporting the oppressed in their efforts to restore their humanity. How might an educational institution and its practices act as an oppressor? What kind of transformative peace education pedagogy might teachers adopt in order to re-humanize those whose humanity has been withheld from them?

9. Learn Lessons about Peaceful Coexistence from Integrated Schools

Northern Ireland, despite the recent transformation to a more peaceful society, remains a society largely segregated with regard to schooling, residential housing, and social activities. In 1981 the first integrated (mixed Catholic and Protestant) school, Lagan College, was established and since then a further sixty-one integrated schools have opened. In a study of the impact of integrated education on two cohorts of former pupils, Claire McGlynn (2001) found a significant long term positive impact on cross-community friendships, respect for diversity, confidence in plural settings, and an enhancement of the ability to empathize with alternative perspectives. Integrated education also appeared to facilitate student exploration of personal and group identities in a non-threatening environment with a subsequent range of impacts on past pupils' perceptions of their social, religious and political identities. Some former students reported that they were "more" Catholic or Protestant as a result of attending an integrated school, others that they were "less" so. Another group reported that they no longer wished to be classified in this way. However a superordinate "integrated identity" was claimed by the majority of these former students and was characterized by respect for diversity, broadmindedness, understanding, and tolerance.

What role do you think that education plays in the development of student identity? How might this role compete with other socializing influences such as family, community, and the media? Rob Reich (2002) suggests that schools should not script for a certain identity, but rather develop student autonomy. How can this be reconciled with a policy of respecting the religious and cultural background of students? Can education help construct a superordinate peaceful identity? What does all of this say about the way in which we conceptualize identity—is it a tangible entity, a social construct, an ever-evolving and fluid notion, something which has multiple facets, or something else?

10. Promote Peace Leadership: Adopt Transformative Values and Capacities

Betty Reardon (1999, 14-15) describes a helpful system of peace values and capacities that need to be fostered in future teachers; it could be argued that these values and capacities are also needed in all peace leaders. The framework includes the value of environmental responsibility, cultural diversity, human solidarity, social responsibility, and gender equality. Corresponding to these values are capacities for transforming societies into cultures of peace: ecological awareness, cultural competency, conflict proficiency, and gender sensitivity.

Individually or in groups, you can begin with self-examination. Write the values of environmental responsibility, cultural diversity, human solidarity, social responsibility, and gender equality on a flip chart, board, or piece of paper. Think of specific behaviors that you or others do that are related to each of the listed values. Identify everyone's strengths as peace leaders according to this value framework. Identify areas for improvement. Discuss the possibilities and constraints for improvement. Complete the above exercise in the context of ecological awareness, cultural competency, conflict proficiency, and gender sensitivity. What behaviors correlate with these capacities? Strengths? Areas of improvement? Develop action plans for peace leadership.

11. Understand the Role of Peace Education

In their seminal book, *Peace Education,* Harris and Morrison (2004) describe an exercise devised by peace scholar Elise Boulding. This exercise is suitable for both adults and children. Establish a "two hundred year present," that is, think back one hundred years to what life was like and think forward one hundred years into the future. What changes have taken place or will take place? Have peace activities been successful; which will be successful? Explore why. This exercise transforms peace educators into action researchers by pushing theory into practice; hopefully those involved become, as Gandhi exhorted, the changes that they wish to see.

Harris and Morrison propose that peace educators should play a critical role in futures education, helping students imagine a better future and uncover the steps needed to get there. The above exercise requires people to imagine a point on the future and then come back ten years and identify the changes needed to realize that future. By going back in intervals of ten years, they are finally brought back to the present, having constructed a series of ten-year plans for progress towards a more peaceful future. In such a way, according to Harris and Morrison, peace education should fundamentally change the way in which people look at the world. This exercise has the possibility of modifying perceptions of the roles that individuals can play in transforming the future. Above all, this exercise offers hope.

Try out this kind of futures exercise. Afterwards explore the barriers that would limit progress and ask for suggestions on how these might be overcome. To what extent might such an exercise discourage people who suffer from inequalities and other forms of structural violence in their daily lives? How can we keep such visioning activities grounded in realism rather than idealism, but also retain the life-giving hope that they offer?

12. Search for Forgiveness as Part of Reconciliation

One critical element of reconciliation deals with the notion of forgiveness, which, at its core, acknowledges the wrongs committed and those harmed, while asking perpetrators to examine their actions and be held accountable. Bishop Desmond Tutu's (1999) *No Future without Forgiveness* describes the central role of forgiveness within South Africa as the Truth and Reconciliation Commission sought to begin healing the deep wounds left by apartheid and help pave the way for a functioning democracy to take hold.

Junior high school teacher Sonia Modesti writes: "In order to begin discussing the topic of forgiveness in an English course, I could ask students to engage in a search for examples of forgiveness in major literary works (prose, poetry, plays). So often, literature focuses on the drama of revenge. Know that this kind of search may prove challenging yet richly rewarding." Find themes of forgiveness in your favorite novels, films, and plays. Have others do the same and discuss your insights.

13. Redefine the Purposes of School and Emphasize Universal Love, Forgiveness, and Reconciliation

Peace scholar and professor Jing Lin (2006) advocates for a global ethic of universal love, forgiveness, and reconciliation; she provides a constructive, optimistic critique of the very purposes of education in the United States and around the world. In her new co-edited book, *Transforming Education for Peace*, Lin (2008) argues for a paradigm shift where the teaching of love comprises the central purpose of education. Lin maintains, "I envision our future schools will shift from a mechanical, functionalistic perspective that primarily emphasizes tests and efficiency, to a constructive, transformative paradigm where students' intellectual, moral, emotional, spiritual, and ecological abilities are developed in order to promote understanding of the world and help nurture love and respect for all human beings and nature. In all, constructing a loving world should be the central purpose of education in the twenty-first century" (315).

Ask everyone to envision the ideal school, community, nation, or world where love serves as the foundational means and ends of education. Describe the curriculum, how teaching is conducted, how people are assessed on their capacities for love, and how the policy context and rule of law shape the containers in which cultural actors engage in everyday loving behaviors.

14. Move Toward a Critical Peace Education

In the *Encyclopedia of Peace Education,* Monisha Bajaj (2008) argues for the reclamation of critical peace education that engages current scholars in efforts toward structural analysis, interrogation of asymmetrical power dynamics, a contextualized understanding of conflict and "historicized knowledge," and emancipatory action toward change; she also advocates for bolstering and complexifying discourses surrounding human rights. Bajaj (2008) maintains, "Moving away from a one-size-fits-all approach toward a contextualized and situated perspective on peace education can only further enhance the legitimacy and validity of the knowledge generated in the field" (143). Her chapter, entitled "Critical Peace Education," situates her current advocacy upon the shoulders of the past praxis scholarship (i.e., theory into practice) of Galtung, Freire, Giroux, Diaz-Soto, Kincheloe, and the like.

Peace education scholar Ed Brantmeier (2007) elaborates on various stages of critical peace education: "Critical peace education, informed by the work of Freire (1970), includes various stages: raising consciousness about various forms of violence (direct, indirect, structural, cultural); imagining nonviolent alternatives (from social, economic, and political structures to psychological and spiritual methods for attaining inner peace); providing specific modes of empowerment (conflict resolution skills, critical thinking, political participation and mobilization, global perspectives and opportunities). . . [Critical] peace education includes enacted plans to move toward a more peaceful and just world through social transformation. The main focus of critical peace education is transformation via consciousness raising, vision, and action. Thus, critical peace education is action-oriented by promoting social and cultural change toward a nonviolent, sustainable, and renewable future" (5-6).

Examine a problem, obstacle, challenge, or conflict that prevents deeper peace at the community, national, or global level. Think about the structural and power dynamics, the historical-contextual underpinnings of the situation, the key players and their spheres of influence, and the policy that enables and/or constrains transformative change. Develop an alternative vision toward reconciliation and peace. Create action plans and then engage in local and wider action toward changing the situation.

15. Join the Dance of Diversity and Unity for Peace

In an effort toward building a robust, and integrative theoretical framework for peace education, H. B. Danesh (2006) advocates for a unity paradigm and provides a typology of worldviews, conceptually defined as "our view of (1) reality, (2) human nature, (3) the purpose of life, and (4) approach to human relationships" (66). Danesh maintains that our worldviews are shaped by our individual life experiences as well as our historically bound, cultural histories—in other words, our worldviews are comprised of individual subjectivities as well as our experiences in groups, communities, and particular contexts. But there is more to the picture. Danesh also posits that there are more universal dimensions of the human experience—"unity, development, creativity" (66)—that transcend social categories of culture, language, race, religion, creed, or ideological conditioning.

The first level in Danesh's typology of worldviews is the *survival-based worldview*, characterized by hierarchical power structures, authoritarianism, and relationships where "power over" people by a ruling elite constitutes conditions that are not conducive to sustainable peace. *Identity-based worldviews* are the second level of evolution—adversarial power structures, extreme competition, and a "survival of the fittest" mentality govern this stage of worldview development. This stage might be encapsulated by the phrase "power over and against in the competition to win." Quite differently, the *unity-based worldview* "requires the application of universal ethical principles at all levels of government and leadership. It ensures that the basic human needs and rights— survival and security; justice, equality, and freedom in all human associations; and the opportunity for a meaningful, generative life—are met within the framework of the rule of law and moral/ethical principles" (68). Cooperative power structures, caring relationships, and universal principles govern this "power with" orientation.

Analyze and categorize the power structures, quality of relationships, and governing principles of your school, college, university, organization, community, or country according to Danesh's worldview typology. Also, discuss the tension between forging unity and affirming diversity in your organization, community, or country. How can you build common or transcendent ground while simultaneously ensuring that processes of assimilation do not squelch the cultural, linguistic, and creative diversity that exists? What are the benefits of unity, the potential pitfalls? What are the benefits of diversity, the potential pitfalls? How can they be harmonized to actualize a sustainable peace?

16. Identify Role Models of Peaceful Right Action

Scott and Helen Nearing's lives personified the path of peaceful right action. Having been released from two major universities for his activism for social justice including child labor laws, Scott and his wife Helen moved to Vermont, and later to Maine, to homestead. Building their own homes out of stone, well into their 70s and 80s, Helen and Scott continued to write and speak for social causes their entire lives. How they lived their lives on a daily basis, however, said as much about their beliefs as their writings. Living very simply off the land and keeping peace with the planet gave them the freedom to choose how they spent their time. This independent spirit carried on even to the end of life.

In her book, *Loving and Leaving the Good Life,* Helen describes the choices Scott made at the end of his life. A month before his 100th birthday, Scott told a group of friends he would no longer be taking food. Although not sick, he felt his body was ready to begin its final transition. Six weeks later, with Helen attending to his needs and his process, Scott passed peacefully from his body in the living room of their home. Scott and Helen serve as amazing examples of taking responsibility for one's life, including all choices and actions, right up until the very end.

Reflect on these questions: What do you think of Scott's decision to make peace with his own life's journey and stop eating? How would you have felt if you were Helen? How are you living out your beliefs about peace and reconciliation on a daily basis? How does this connect to your being a role model for right action?

17. Research Female Role Models of Peace

Many of the traditional role models for peace in our curricula have been males, such as Gandhi and Dr. Martin Luther King, Jr. Presenting female role models who are living their values and ideals of peace on a daily basis is important for all of our students, female and male. Jane Goodall and Aung San Suu Kyi are just two of the current female peace pilgrims that Nathalie Kees likes to discuss in her university counseling classes.

"I share Jane Goodall's story through her video *Reason for Hope: A Spiritual Journey.* By viewing this video, students see a woman in her 70s, who is still traveling and speaking close to 300 days per year, sharing with students her belief that we can all make a difference in the condition of our planet and its inhabitants, human and animal. She discusses her pain as she witnessed the periods of violence between groups of chimpanzees, having hoped that the chimps were a more peaceful and innocent version of ourselves. She also outlines concrete ways for students to become involved in improving conditions for animals and humans through her 'Roots and Shoots' projects in schools and shares a variety of success stories from all over the world. Her indefatigable energy and daily mission to create a non-violent world where resources are shared make her a truly inspiring role model.

"Aung San Suu Kyi, the democratically elected leader of Burma (Myanmar) and recipient of the 1991 Nobel Peace Prize, has been living under surveillance and/or house arrest for almost two decades. Although the government has told her she is free to leave the country, she knows that she will not be allowed to return. Therefore, she stays and works for a peaceful and democratic solution to the military takeover of Burma, even during the illness and death of her husband in England in 1999. Her conversations with Alan Clements have been recorded in the audiocassette *The Voice of Hope: Conversations with Aung San Suu Kyi.*"

What do these two women have in common with some other women you know? How are they similar to or different from you? What steps might their actions inspire you to take on behalf of peace?

18. Learn about the Peace Pilgrim (1908-1981)

So often in our educational systems, the canon of women's history has to be recovered by each new generation of scholars. Nathalie Kees insists that this has "definitely been true for me as I have searched for female role models of peace. I have only recently been introduced to one of the founding mothers of the peace movement, Peace Pilgrim. Born Mildred Norman on July 18, 1908, she took the name Peace Pilgrim in her mid-forties. After many years of physical, spiritual, and emotional preparation, she began walking across the United States in 1953, without possessions or money, 'until mankind learns the way of peace.' From 1953 until her death in 1981, she walked across the United States seven times on pilgrimages for peace. She chose not to eat until food was offered to her, or sleep until shelter was provided. Her message was simple, 'Here is the way of peace: Overcome evil with good, falsehood with truth, and hatred with love'" (Peace Pilgrim, *Steps Toward Inner Peace*).

Peace Pilgrim's writings have been maintained by the "Friends of Peace Pilgrim" and are available, free of charge, from this group. A documentary of her life, entitled, *Peace Pilgrim: An American Sage Who Walked Her Talk,* provides an excellent 60 minute introduction to her life and work and is also available, along with other videos and books of her life's work, from the Friends of Peace Pilgrim at www.peacepilgrim.org.

After viewing these materials, reflect on the following: What world events happened during Peace Pilgrim's formative years, between 1908 and 1953, that influenced her decision to walk for peace? What kinds of physical, spiritual, and emotional preparations did it take for her to get ready to walk?

One decision Peace Pilgrim made was to completely balance her needs and wants. She believed there was nothing she needed that she didn't have and that you couldn't give her anything she didn't need. If you gave her anything, even something as small as a postage stamp, that she didn't need, she felt that it would be a burden to her. She decided to "live simply so that others could simply live." Ask yourself: How balanced are the wants and needs of your life? How do our choices affect the lives of others in the world? How is everyone interconnected? Although Peace Pilgrim's life may seem extraordinary, she considered herself a very ordinary person. How might her actions inspire you?

19. Understand How Memories Can Undermine Reconciliation

In December 1983, in a small town in Northern Ireland, sectarian tensions between Protestants and Catholics were running high. It was a time when loss of life through bombing and shooting was a sadly routine event. That December the local Catholic church was burned in an arson attack by loyalist (Protestant) sympathizers and in a brave gesture of reconciliation, a local Protestant minister walked across to what was left of the Catholic church and held out his hand to wish the Catholic priest a "Merry Christmas." A very small but significant reaching out to show support and solidarity to a fellow human being, you might think. What the minister did not anticipate was the wave of fury that ensued. Vilified by loyalists as a traitor, the minister and his family were subjected to a prolonged campaign of intimidation, despite the unwavering support of the Catholic priest. In real danger of his life, and after receiving a coffin with his name on it, the Protestant minister was forced out of the area by the sectarian bigots.

Twenty five years later, in September 2008, a local councillor put forward a motion to honor the minister (and his Catholic counterpart) with the freedom of the town, stating that he was a "man ahead of his time" in terms of peace-building in Northern Ireland. That motion was unanimously defeated by fellow councillors who argued, not of course on sectarian grounds, but on the rather shaky assertion that this was "unfair," and they would need to honor all clergy and not single out individuals. *Plus ça change, plus c'est la même chose...*

What does this real life story teach us about the challenges to reconciliation in deeply divided societies? What does it teach us about how bias and bigotry are transmitted across the generations? What kinds of peace-making interventions might interrupt these processes?

20. Teach about Threat and Challenge

Teaching about peace and reconciliation can upset those who are quick to see disloyalty in dissent. Others see themselves fulfilling their patriotic duty when they challenge an authority they see going wrong. There are parallels in other areas. In *Teaching Diversity,* for example, Silvia Canetto and Evelinn Borrayo (2003) describe the challenges and threats for students who look at issues of power and powerlessness, privilege and prejudice, those places where society in general struggles to untangle emotions and ideas from historic oppressions, injustices, and biases. As with teaching about peace and reconciliation, expertise and skilled facilitation are essential.

Canetto and Borrayo write: "Teaching about human diversity is exciting. It engages students and instructors with scientifically rich and personally meaningful issues such as gender, sexual orientation, ethnicity, or social class. It involves participating in a journey that can be intellectually and personally transforming. At the same time, teaching about human diversity is challenging. . . (However, for) many students, learning about social stratification and inequalities is threatening because it challenges their assumptions about other people and about themselves, as well as their reasons for their places in the world. For example, for some students it may be personally challenging to consider that achievement is not simply a function of merit. Some react to threatening content through denial and resistance. Feelings of shame, guilt, anxiety, and anger also maybe triggered. In some instances, students turn their negative feelings against the instructor who becomes the target of hostility" (189-190).

Reflect on moments when you have felt threatened or challenged in the classroom. What feelings have you had when you've learned or taught some aspect of peace and reconciliation that was deeply uncomfortable and challenged your worldview? When was it most challenging? Threatening to you or others? What has helped channel strong feelings into growth and development?

BEING PEACE

Gandhi celebrated the value of meditation for focusing on peace and sustaining a commitment to nonviolence, both inwardly and outwardly, on "being the change we wish to see." On a very practical level, staying centered in times of crisis is a central component of both anger management and stress reduction. It is hard for anyone to communicate sensitively when emotions run high. Being peace is part and parcel of doing peace. In that light, being peace is something that needs to be cultivated when teaching, learning, doing peace, and promoting reconciliation.

21. Perk Up, Lean In, and Stay Centered

Difficult times can provide essential lessons. Noted Buddhist nun and author, Pema Chodron (1994), has some ideas about staying present to what is happening, that this very moment can be the "perfect teacher." She writes: "Most of us do not take these moments as teachings. . . [Moments like this can] teach us to perk up and lean in when we feel we'd rather collapse and back away."

Sonja Modesti splits her teaching between a junior high school and speech classes at the university. One of her biggest challenges has been "Susie," who jumped off the edge of respectable behavior and dived into very risky experimentation with drugs, alcohol and sex, all at the tender age of fifteen—despite coming from a seemingly normal, middle class home with two professional parents. On the very first day of class, Sonja touched Susie on the shoulder when passing by her desk at which time Susie said for all to hear: "Don't ever put you f***ing hands on me again, or I'm calling the police and claiming assault."

Over time—when Susie was in class—Sonja made some progress in creating a relationship, coaxing out the occasional shock story that got the desired attention. Sonja asked and then listened if she got a response. She empathized, problem-solved, challenged, and pleaded. Just what any caring teacher would do. She even went so far as to invite Susie to hang out with her. At one point, life got so bad at home for Susie that Sonja invited her to move in with her, but Susie's parents refused. The question that Sonja raised was about staying free of labels like "at-risk" when dealing with the Susie's of this world. Those kinds of labels offered no help, just a predetermined category. What did seem to help was to stay free of any such judgments and, instead, stay present and continue to build some kind of relationship. Susie was earning Cs in her coursework, a dramatic improvement from the past, when she did little, if anything. What also helped was not to panic, to run from Susie or sink into despair, or just to give up completely. From reading the few papers she handed in, Sonja knew that Susie was very bright and expressive, though often lost in her own rebellion.

Pema Chodron continues: "Meditation is an invitation to notice when we reach our limit and to not get carried away by hope or fear. Through meditation, we're able to see clearly what's going on with our thoughts and emotions, and we can also let them go. What's encouraging about meditation is that even if we shut down, we can no longer shut down in ignorance" (14).

Describe a time when someone else's situation seemed bleak and beyond repair. What were your thoughts and feelings? Imagine what you could have learned from this experience? What do you do to stay centered in times of crisis? Identify what you could do. Speculate on how meditation could help?

22. Overcome Prejudice and Practice Loving-Kindness Meditation

Prejudices inevitably trigger tensions and conflicts. Loving-kindness meditation, however, a practice rooted in the Buddhist tradition, can help diminish the negative associations we may have for certain people through a process that neutralizes these negative emotions and then extends loving-kindness to all, both friend and foe.

With eyes closed, ask people to think of themselves in a loving way by focusing on their positive attributes. Then, ask them to envision someone they are fond of—someone they love very much. Maybe a sense of caring, gratitude, respect, or kindness might emerge. Ask them to extend loving-kindness toward that person. Then, ask them to think of someone they view neutrally, without much emotive association, and cultivate a sense of loving-kindness toward that person. Then, ask them to consider someone they view as an enemy, a foe, or otherwise undesirable, and extend loving-kindness to this person as well. In this way, non-differentiation among friend, neutral, and enemy is cultivated, and loving-kindness and compassion can be extended unconditionally to all—through practice.

23. Find Peace Within: A Guided Meditation

As a graduate student, Lisa Barrett came to believe that peace in the world comes from within. She maintains that we cannot create peace if we don't have it ourselves, in our hearts and in our homes. She encourages people to try this exercise: Choose a word that is special to them; one that has a peaceful meaning for the world around them. Play soft music and maintain low lighting if possible. The facilitator should read the following, allowing for pauses as appropriate:

Come to a comfortable seated position. If you prefer to lie on the floor, please do so. If you are sitting, create length in the spine. Imagine it is your connection between the earth and sky. Allow your eyes to close. Begin with a deep inhale, and release. Allow your breath to return to normal. Observe the sounds around you. Become aware of all the sound you may hear—the breathing of the person next to you, the heater (or air conditioner), any birds, sounds of cars. . . (Pause here for a long moment to allow members to become aware of their environment.)

Become aware of your body. Observe where the clothes touch your body and how they feel against your body. Observe where your body touches the chair. Observe where your arms make contact with your body. Identify any areas of tension within the body. With each exhale, allow those areas to relax. (Pause here.)

Observe the face. Squeeze all the muscles within the face, and then allow them to relax with your next exhale. Observe the throat, which is the connection between the heart and mind. Move the head from side to side to release any tension. (Pause here for a long moment to allow members to bring awareness to their body.)

Become aware of your breath. Observe the natural rhythm of inhaling and exhaling. Observe the air as it is inhaled through the nose; it is cooler. Now observe the warmth of the breath as it is exhaled. (Pause here for a few moments.). . . Observe the breath within the chest and stomach. Take a big inhale, filling the stomach with air. Observe how the stomach releases. Next fill the lungs with air and release.

Begin to silently repeat the special word you have chosen. Combine it with the in breath. Hear the word whispered as the breath comes in. As the breath leaves, allow the special word to flow out as a wish to the world. Keep the mind focused and allow the special word to draw you inward, to embrace each part of the body and mind. (Four minute long pause.)

Slowly and gently, begin to increase the inhalation. . . . (Pause.) As you exhale, begin to whisper softly your wish of peace to the world. Slowly and gently allow the eyes to open and behold the first rays of light. Continue to slowly open the eyes, and allow the light from within to shine out into the world. Wishing all peace. (Devi 1994)

24. Think Peace with Every Step and Raise Awareness

Buddhist monk and peace activist, Thich Nhat Hanh (1991), gained fame during the Vietnam War by calling for all combatants, on both sides of the war, to end the killing and destruction. Since that time he has championed "mindfulness" activities as a way to stay centered in the midst of crisis.

In *Being Peace,* Thich Nhat Hanh (1996) also asks whether we can foster the capacity to look with eyes that see ourselves in one another, becoming more aware of and sensitive to others and the earth that we share. He answers his own question with an original poem which reflects on the nature of suffering in life, considering, among several examples, the starving child whose hunger might be abated were it not for her nation's use of its funds to buy weaponry. Nhat Hanh asks that in our seeing the realities of the world around us—even in the extraordinary pain and suffering of a starving child—that we find it within ourselves to call one another by our "true names," his request made in the closing lines of his poem:

> Please call me by my true names,
> so I can hear all my cries and laughs at once,
> so I can see that my joy and pain are one.
>
> Please call me by my true names,
> so I can wake up,
> and so the door of my heart can be left open,
> the door of compassion. (64)

Working with the honors program at the University of Northern Colorado, Debra Kaye Holman organizes events to link students with issues beyond campus boundaries. She writes: "As (Nhat Hanh) points out, to be known by our true names implies recognition of our interconnectedness with and responsibility to one another. By seeing with eyes capable of acknowledging the pain and suffering in the world, we are additionally challenged to foster compassion toward each other. A greater challenge, though, lies not just in the recognition of the state of the world, but also in the consideration of our own actions to help reduce the suffering in which we all share."

To raise awareness and see these connections, have people take a mindfulness walk, outside if possible. With each step with the left foot, they say, *"I teach peace."* With each step of the right foot, they say, *"I teach reconciliation."* Some will report how unusual it is to walk so slowly and NOT have a destination and ETA (Estimated Time of Arrival). Others will realize how they already are teaching peace and reconciliation in some way. Unaccustomed to this kind of inner self-discipline, some may be distracted. Regular practice may lead to additional insights.

You can also think about the role that government plays. Look into a specific situation that is of concern to you and then write a letter to your Congressional representative or senators to help bring attention to that issue. Act within your own sphere of influence to support initiatives aimed at improving the lives of others. By learning more about organizations such as One Laptop per Child (http://laptop.org/), which seeks to expand educational opportunities for children around the world, you may even find yourself drawn to engage in activities in which you can actively play a role in reducing the suffering.

25. Counteract Compassion Fatigue with Tonglen Practice

The impact of violence and its associated traumas goes beyond the victims. Compassion fatigue is one outcome of the secondary trauma that teachers and counselors can experience as they work with and/or hear the stories of children and adults traumatized by violence (Kees and Lashwood 1996). Compassionate helpers often carry this secondary trauma in their emotional and physical bodies, unaware of the damage it might be causing them. Likely outcomes include illness, burn-out, rash or reactive judgments or actions, or hardening of the heart and inability to continue listening to the difficulties of others.

Tonglen (Chodron 1994, 2001) is a Buddhist practice of opening the heart, breathing in the dark or traumatic feelings and emotions of another, allowing ourselves to completely feel these feelings with a compassionate heart, and then transforming these feelings as we breathe out, releasing the feelings as positive energy for the other and all other beings experiencing similar feelings or trauma. This practice allows us to become a compassionate witness to the experience of the other, helping to relieve the isolation and suffering of the other, and helping to determine the right and appropriate actions.

Become comfortable with this practice yourself before working with others. Allow yourself to relax quietly, becoming aware of your breath. Allow your heart to open. Become aware of feelings of pain or suffering that you or someone close to you has felt. Allow yourself to breath in this dark and painful energy, feeling it fully and completely. As you breathe out, imagine transforming this dark energy into a cool, white, light that you are able to send out to others and to the world. This increased awareness allows us to stay open as compassionate listeners for others.

26. Being Peace: Walking the Labyrinth

The labyrinth is an ancient method of pilgrimage designed for the poor person who could not afford to travel to distant pilgrimage sites. Lauren Artress (2006) has spent her life bringing the labyrinth to the United States and facilitating individuals and groups as they experience the labyrinth's path toward inner and collective peace. The metaphors hidden within the labyrinth walk provide a rich source of awareness related to internal and external peace. For example, a labyrinth differs from a maze in that the labyrinth has one path in and out, while the maze has one right path and many dead ends. In the world of peace education, we can find commonalities along the one path we all seek, versus finding, fighting over, and convincing each other in our attempts to find the one "right" path in the maze, all the while not realizing we have gone down a dead end.

Find a local labyrinth for you or your group to walk. Some churches, health centers, and hospice organizations have built them and allow for community use. Or create your own. You can find labyrinth kits at Dr. Artress's website: www.veriditas.org.

After the experience of walking the labyrinth, create a discussion around the following questions: What did you experience as you walked in toward the center of the labyrinth? As you returned out from the center? What metaphors for your own inner peace became apparent as you walked? What metaphors for inter-group conflict, negotiation, or mediation did you notice? How might you take this experience of the labyrinth into your personal life? How might you take this experience into your work?

27. Explore Pacifism

After the attacks of September 11th, 2001 in the U.S. and the drumbeat for revenge was sounded ever louder for throwing the full force of American military might against the "evil doers" wherever they hid, Bill Timpson began to join with Quakers/Friends for their Sunday meetings. "As I tried to sort out what I would teach in my classes—just what does an educator say?—I found myself drawn to those faith communities who were committed pacifists, crystal clear that violence of any sort was not an option. I tried the Mennonites in town, but was really drawn to the essential silence of the Quakers/Friends meetings, where I could find the space to meditate on the meaning of peace in the midst of outrage and the build up to war."

When he later worked on *Teaching and Learning Peace,* Timpson (2002) found himself repeatedly returning to the question of nonviolence in Europe during the 1930s, the rise of Hitler and the brutality of the Nazi ascension to power. "Could I be a pacifist in the face of that kind of threat? My dad had volunteered to fight in the Spanish Civil War in 1936–1938, and then later with Patton's U.S. Third Army to rid the world of fascism. Certainly World War Two fit the notion of a 'just war.' The responses I got from my Quaker colleagues really pushed my thinking. What would have happened, they asked, if the allies had committed to a whole range of nonviolent interventions including an economic embargo on Germany and its fascist leaders? Years later we saw the results when the world united to isolate the South African government and its brutally racist policies of apartheid. Several international businesses pulled their operations out. College campuses in the U.S. rang with student voices calling for divestiture of funds from companies doing business with South Africa. Sporting teams from South Africa were barred from participating in international events. No armed invasion was needed; in fact, just the opposite happened. In the face of international pressures, South Africa moved toward inclusion of the black majority in democratic elections and the end of apartheid."

Find a pacifist faith community where you live and attend one of their services or meetings. Read the arguments for nonviolence in the writings and speeches of Gandhi and Martin Luther King, Jr. Join with others to examine the role of pacifism today.

DOING PEACE

In order to be agents of change, to help people and organizations move away from violence and toward constructive conflict resolution, away from privileged hierarchy and toward an appreciative and just inclusion of diversity, we must understand the complexities of peace and how each of us can best contribute. The phrase "doing peace" assumes engaged action in promoting nonviolent, sustainable futures.

28. Understand the Types of Peace Education

Though surely there are more explicit and implicit forms of peace education, Ian Harris (1999) identifies five main types of peace education: (1) global peace education, (2) conflict resolution, (3) violence prevention, (4) developmental education, and (5) nonviolence education (308-309). Each of these types of peace education addresses different forms of violence, such as interstate war, interpersonal violence, street crime, ecological insecurity, structural violence, and enemy stereotyping—to name just a few. According to Harris's typology, each type of peace education has corresponding goals, strategies, and curriculum that can be implemented in schools or community education settings as positive responses to violent situations.

Identify the type of peace education that most closely aligns with your current goals or activism. Research that particular type of peace education to understand these sub-fields in complex, integrated, nuanced, and applied ways. Identify the unique challenges and dynamics of the situations that others face. How could you design needs assessment protocols, intervention plans, and evaluation systems that would be helpful?

29. Study Lessons from a Divided Society Moving toward Peace

Northern Ireland continues to offer hope to countries suffering from seemingly intractable conflict. Claire McGlynn writes: "In April 2008 we celebrated 10 years since the signing of the Good Friday Agreement, in which a constitutional model was agreed upon by nationalists and loyalists. It is important to reflect on how the conflict was resolved and how society can best absorb the lessons learned. We are reflecting on critical aspects of the peace process, not claiming a blueprint for conflict resolution that can be exported elsewhere in the world, but beginning to identify principles that may be helpful. While acknowledging the importance of a range of factors including leadership, the role of third parties (such as the United States), the new constitutional model and the war-weariness of the paramilitary groups, tribute can also be paid to bottom up leadership and to the brave peacemakers who were willing to cross borders in order to hold together a tentative middle ground.

"The main challenge in Northern Ireland is to transform from a society now enjoying negative peace into one that reflects positive peace. There is a legacy of suffering and the thorny issue of how best to honor the victims and to heal the pain, which is tangible. While the overall death toll (some 3,500 dead) appears small, in relation to the population size it is highly significant and most people know someone killed or injured. Emerging accounts of security force collusion in atrocities are painful. The first ever civic action has been brought against bombers, who have thus far evaded justice. To-date there is no formal truth recovery process, only strategies such as healing through remembering are enacted. While the majority of school age children can only remember peace, their families and communities remain deeply affected, and this clearly impacts upon young people. Paramilitary organizations, while proscribed, continue to blight lives, particularly those of young people, who are very much aware of where it is and where it is not safe to go."

Ask these questions: To what extent are experiences of conflict resolution from other countries useful to our own situations? What kind of lessons might emerge from the study of countries such as Northern Ireland? How can we develop theoretical concepts such as "negative" peace and "positive" peace to accommodate the complexities of societies in transition to and from conflict? What is the role of education in a post-conflict society? (See Galtung and Jacobson 2000.)

PEACE KEEPING

As utilized by the United Nations, "peace keepers" play an essential role in separating combatants and others who are in conflict so that the blood-letting can stop long enough for "cooler heads" to prevail and find other, nonviolent ways to resolve conflicts. A range of ideas and skills can be taught and learned to "keep the peace." Peacekeeping at the macro level may involve United Nations efforts or international coalitions providing safety, security, and humanitarian needs within a given conflict zone; it is a form of deterrence violence (Whaley and Piazza-Georgi 1997). Peacekeeping at the micro-level may involve keeping communities and institutions secure and safe. It often takes the form of police patrols and community watch groups who attempt to create violence free neighborhoods and public spaces.

30. It Is Our Job to Transform Conflict

In *The Third Side*, renowned mediator Bill Ury (2000) describes his tour of a Strategic Air Command (SAC) facility and aircraft where the guide insisted that it was not the job of the Department of Defense to communicate with the Russians should a conflict arise. "It's the job of the State Department." Ury goes on to explain why he has such a problem with this kind of deflection of responsibility. "The same attitude of 'not our job' is pervasive when it comes to dealing with the destructive conflicts around us. Our first instinct when a dispute erupts is often to stand aside on the grounds that it is none of our business. Or we take sides. Either way, we contribute to the escalation of the conflict. To paraphrase Edmund Burke, 'the only thing necessary for the triumph of force is for good people to do nothing'" (23).

List five conflicts that you find disturbing. Now prioritize what you have put on your list from "Most Disturbing" (#5) to "Least Disturbing" (#1). Score each conflict according to the following:

- Which conflicts can you impact: Rate from "High" to "Some" to "None"?
- Where can you see a "Third Side," neither "For" nor "Against"?
- Which should you avoid: i.e., "It's None of My Business"?

Individually, or in small groups, compare responses and think about how these conflicts could be transformed in the future.

31. Question the Conflict-Education Connection

In *Earth in Mind,* David Orr (1994) decries the loss of habitat and species, and raises questions about the nature of a school system that would allow that loss to occur. He then goes on to raise the same question about education's role in allowing atrocities against humans. "It is worth noting that this is not the work of people with BAs, LLBs, MBAs, and PhDs. Elie Wiesel once made the same point, noting that the designers and perpetrators of Auschwitz, Dachau, and Buchenwald—the Holocaust—were the heirs of Kant and Goethe, widely thought to be the best educated people on earth. But their education did not serve as an adequate barrier to barbarity. What was wrong with their education?" (7).

List five conflicts, including some that are political and some that are personal. Now identify one educational component for each. Then offer one curricular recommendation that you think would make a difference and give people at least one idea that they would need to handle these conflicts more skillfully. This is a tall order, to move in some situations from a large and public issue to a specific curricular recommendation, but we need to start somewhere. For example, handling waste is a problem that besets many communities and industries. There are potentially useful "molecules" and much embodied energy in whatever is thrown away that could be recycled or reused. Landfills are also costly to maintain. Cardboard and plastic packaging is often added for purposes of shipping, storage, advertising and/or protection against theft. As a curricular issue, you could begin with some knowledge about the nature and costs of waste, noting that there is no "waste" in nature. At an analytical level, you could connect various wars and conflicts to competition over resources. At another level, you could evaluate a sample of waste from a local landfill and trace the contents to their sources for manufacturing. At an application level, you could then guide the development of a public relations program to raise awareness and change behavior.

32. Retake Ownership of Conflicts

Norwegian criminologist Nils Christie introduced to the Western world the idea that ownership of conflicts was taken away from people by the crown or government. He argued that before William the Conqueror, people were responsible for their own conflicts, and after he took over as King of England people lost this ownership right (Christie 1977). His work helped form the basis for what we now know as restorative justice.

To this day in the Western world criminal cases are brought in the name of the state, nation, or crown. This loss of ownership of conflicts is believed to have affected how we view conflicts in every setting, not just in the courts. In the Western world, we tend to avoid conflict, seek elimination of conflict, or rely on an expert to solve the problem, rather than accepting that conflicts are inevitable and building our capacity to resolve conflicts non-violently. This idea applies to schools, and often we find teachers would rather refer problem be-haviors in the classroom on to others, who are seen as experts in dealing with misbehaviors, or at least those with the responsibility to do so.

The question educators and those interested in education can ask them-selves is what skills can I learn so that, rather than avoiding conflict, I can re-spond to conflict in a healthy way?

33. Remove Weapons

If we are serious about promoting peace, we should work to reduce gun related deaths and accidents. One strategy that noted mediator Bill Ury (1999) advocates is quite simple and direct: remove guns. "One way to stop people from using dangerous weapons against each other is to take them away. In Great Britain, the annual murder rate stands at one per hundred thousand peo-ple, while in the United States the rate is at least eight times higher. One power-ful reason is that firearms, tightly controlled in Britain, are plentiful and easily available in America. The death rate among American children is nearly sixteen times higher than among children in twenty-five other industrialized countries combined. Far from 'fight-proof,' American society remains tragically 'fight-prone'" (180).

Ury goes on to offer a concrete example of community support for lower-ing gun violence through removal of dangerous weapons. "To combat teen ho-micide in Boston in the 1990s, the Boston Gun Project sought to keep guns out of the hands of youths. Researchers at Harvard University provided information about the kinds of guns used by teenagers, and government officials then devel-oped strategies for tracking down and arresting suppliers of these types of guns. The project also established a program to buy back guns from teenagers. Backed by the community, the police rigorously enforced firearms restrictions and the county imposed heavy sentences on offenders. The collaboration among residents, government agencies, and the community worked. In 1996, no youths under seventeen died from handgun violence; and homicide rates for people under twenty-four had dropped by three-quarters from the 1990 num-bers. The successful initiative has now spread to at least seventeen other cities. Hiding the poisoned arrows helps" (180). Any of us could examine the connec-tions between youth and violence in our own communities and lobby to "hide whatever poisoned arrows" are implicated.

Know that in the U.S. there is a fierce opposition to any form of gun con-trol. The National Rifle Association, in particular, is very active politically in pro-tecting what they see as the sanctity of the constitutional protection for the "right to bear arms." Question: just how do you limit access to dangerous weap-ons and support the rights of citizens to own arms? Other democratic nations have managed to do both. For example, Scandinavian countries have active hunting clubs where citizens have access to rifles, yet their gun-related murder rates per capita are only a fraction of what exists in the U.S.

PEACEMAKING

Peacemaking has been established as a mechanism for overcoming hierarchy, power, and status when addressing conflicts and tensions. At its core, peacemaking puts everyone on an equal footing as a way to cut through historic and cultural barriers to full, equal, and open participation. Peacemaking at the macro level can be understood as efforts to bring nation-states or groups within a country into dialogue processes toward reconciliation (Whaley and Piazza-Georgi 1997). Peacemaking at the micro level can be understood as mediation of conflict between individuals or groups within local institutions and communities; people can also make peace with the planet that sustains them.

34. Honor the Wisdom of the Peacemaking Circle and the Way of Council

In *Teaching and Learning Peace*, Bill Timpson (2002) connects what we know about instruction with ideas and strategies that underlie efforts toward peace and reconciliation. Having groups meet in a circle, for example, can help build a positive, more inclusive experience. "James Treat is a Native American professor who puts his classes in a circle whenever he can. He wants the connectedness this kind of room arrangement provides. Discussions are better, livelier, when students can see each other. However, it's more than that for Treat because the circle represents an important cultural tradition, one that respects everyone's contributions. Straight rows facing the front put the responsibility on one person to lead. The community becomes hierarchical. The physical design of our classes and how we organize instruction can help connect us with our students and them with each other. This is one of the many ways that attention to the classroom environment builds a foundation that is crucially important for maximizing learning and promoting peacemaking" (50).

While the size of the group makes a difference, there are many creative ways to help people see each other even in large meetings. When a theater is designed "in the round," for example, audience members often feel a greater intimacy with the performers since they are on average closer to the action of the play. Another way is the "fishbowl" technique, in which some members of a large group can be brought to the front of a hall to sit in a circle and demonstrate a certain process while the rest of the audience observes.

Viviane Ephraimson-Abt is the Assistant Director of Apartment Life at Colorado State University and a leader in mediation practice in the local community. She has also studied the use of the circle as "Council" and writes: "Since its formation in 1979, The *Way of Council* has been the central community practice at The Ojai Foundation in Ojai, California. At first glance, council seems like a simple and universal practice. In a circle, folks share their stories by passing around a talking piece. Talking circles like these can be found in many traditional cultures (such as the Native American and Hawaiian) which use sitting in the presence of one another, speaking authentically, and listening attentively to establish and maintain relationships and build community. Yet, many find that the practice of council is a profound way to establish the conditions for peace because it allows each person's truth to be expressed and to be heard in a way that is deeply respectful. Council creates a collective awareness that helps build strong connections and allows differences to co-exist in ways that benefit everyone involved.

"In the *Way of Council*, participants sit in a circle with a prepared center, which usually contains some flowers, a candle or water, and a talking piece. Two (ideally) trained facilitators invite a dedication of the council, introduce the theme, select a talking piece, choose a council form, and then, after everyone has had the opportunity to share, close the council. *A Way of Council* facilitator completes a series of trainings and practices council on a regular basis. Facilitators learn how to prepare the group for council, to develop and introduce themes, to "read the field"—that is, what is happening in the circle, when to use various forms of council, and common concerns that arise from this practice.

"In order to prepare participants, facilitators often lead a series of activities designed to help members become acquainted and to develop trust and the ability to listen deeply and speak authentically. Preparation also includes developing group norms about what is shared in council. For example, agreements are made around confidentiality so that everyone knows what can be shared inside and outside of the circle.

"As described in the book by the same name, *The Way of Council* is guided by four intentions. First, the person with the talking piece *speaks from the heart,* sharing what is personally meaningful in as honest a way as possible. Second, the rest of the participants *listen from the heart* for what is meaningful for the speaker. Third, communication is *spontaneous*, rather than rehearsed. (It is understood that there are times when silence may be the most spontaneous and authentic contribution from the person with the talking piece.) Fourth, *lean expression* is encouraged so that the speaker says only as much as is necessary to be understood and serve the full circle.

"As a council begins, participants are often invited to sit in silence for a few minutes until one person feels inspired to come forward to dedicate the council with a few words and either a lighting of a candle, pouring of water, or another ritual. Alternatively, the council may begin with a song or other shared musical experience. Then the council theme is introduced by the facilitators and a talking piece is used throughout the practice, so that only one person speaks at a time. After everyone has had the opportunity to share, the facilitators may move on to another theme or close the council with a reminder of the opening intention."

The Way of Council has been used by business, community, and educational organizations to improve human relations, to promote understanding between diverse people, even in highly conflicted situations, and to build community. For example, after 9/11/2001, Colorado State University's Apartment Life held councils for international and US students to reduce some of the intense fear that arose at that time. This experience was so beneficial that staff and student leaders became trained in the *Way of Council* and this has been an ongoing practice since then (Skog 2004, 143-145). Also the Los Angeles Unified School District (LAUSD) piloted the *Way of Council* in select junior high schools due to cross-cultural and group conflict. At one of these schools, a 1996-7 study showed that council led to higher grade point averages, improved human relations skills, and a reduction in conflict (Palms Middle School 1997). Council has become strongly embedded in several schools in the LAUSD (Whitney 2007) and now there is a central office in LAUSD devoted entirely to the implementation of council in Los Angeles Schools.

Council programs inspired by the work at The Ojai Foundation are now ongoing in many parts of the US and the world, including Europe, Africa, and Israel. Bringing council into your community is easy. Check their website: http://www.ojaifoundation.org.

Analyze a recent meeting that was organized in the more traditional manner of audience facing the stage or podium. Now analyze another meeting that was organized in a circle. What was different? How has the circle helped you resolve conflicts, heal differences, and find constructive ways forward? Adopt the *Way of Council* for several meetings and discuss its impact. Experiment with the use of a "talking stick" to increase participation and provide new "spaces" for deeper and heart-felt communication.

35. Reframe Disruptions as Opportunities to Build Peacemaking Capacities

School violence is often the subject of media coverage and political concern. Calls for getting tough and zero tolerance are the responses we hear. However, these approaches to wrongdoing and conflict in schools do little to build the capacity of students to respond to these situations non-violently. Just as many teachers have learned to replace their traditional chalk-and-talk approaches to teaching in the classroom with more discursive strategies, they also adopt a more co-constructed and power sharing approach to problems related to student behavior. Rather than seeing these behaviors as disruptions to learning, they can be viewed as learning opportunities.

One way to respond to wrongdoing and conflict is by using circle processes (Pranis 2005). These processes build healthy and caring relationships, improve communications, and change the culture of a school. These circles provide students and teachers opportunities to learn and practice social skills, listening, empathy, problem solving, conflict resolution, anger management, and expression of feelings. By using a talking piece with the clear expectation that the piece will go around the circle in order, students and teachers learn to listen and reflect before they speak.

Tom Cavanagh has studied restorative practices for many years, including several years in New Zealand working with Maori communities. He writes: "I recommend that teachers and their students learn more about circles and begin using circles at the opening of class as a transition from one context to another so that they can unload the baggage they bring with them and be able to focus on the learning."

36. Learn from Others Who Have Experience with Violence

In *Long Shadows,* Cold War veteran Don Kliese (2006) remembers being stationed in Germany during the 1980s, when international tensions between East and West were high, when the "sword rattling" between the U.S. and the U.S.S.R., in particular, was intense and unnerving, when national security was encased within a nuclear arms race, and talk of "mutually assured destruction" was at the core of U.S. defense thinking. As an infantryman, Kliese often patrolled the border between East and West Germany, at times a few feet apart from East German troops. Yet, he remembers how kind the German people were, the horrors of their own experience in war so very recent and raw. "They always expressed such a deep sadness to see young men such as us primed for war. They had lived it. They lived it in such ways that we could never even begin to comprehend. So many of them were really sad and angry. They would say to us: 'We don't want to see you live what we did, and we're so afraid that's what's going to happen again.' . . . It's a mixed feeling when you serve in the military. It's that sense of pride of having served, but also a sense of despair about what you did" (254).

Many scholars believe that the televised images of the Vietnam War had much to do with the eventual decline in U.S. public support and why the Pentagon has been so intent on managing the news coming out of subsequent wars and military operations. When have you seen the devastation of war? How did it affect you? Others? How can the "experience" of war be built into the education we need for promoting peace and reconciliation? Can we make better use of film clips, documentaries, and theater productions? Atwood Publishing has produced a DVD of several of these veterans speaking about their contributions to the *Long Shadows* book. Visit their website and look under "Bookshelf" and "Social Justice" (http://www.atwoodpublishing.com/).

37. Dig for a Deeper Peace

In *Teaching Diversity,* Jim Banning (2003) draws parallels between what he would like to see in the way of a "deeper" commitment to diversity, policies, and practices that go beyond the "surface" celebrations of this or that group, and what ecologists mean about going "deeper" to address the demands of burgeoning human populations and their collective appetite for "stuff." He wants us to look at our shared environment and the inherent limits of our natural resources. The same arguments could be made for peace and reconciliation.

Banning writes:

Ecological problems from the 'deep' perspective are seen as being woven into the complexity of our worldviews, philosophies, spirituality, and the way we see ourselves. They are not problems that technological tinkering can resolve... (208)

In deep diversity, the classroom struggle will be recognized, support will be given, context will be included in classroom/teacher evaluations, scholarship surrounding the experience will be valued, and students will find support of diversity not only in their diversity classes but also in other classes, in their residence halls, in institutional policy, and on the bricks and mortar of the campus (215).

Evaluate various efforts that contribute toward peace and reconciliation with this lens of what's "surface" and what's "deep." Brainstorm ways in which, for example, the energy and creativity that are often invested in a one-time demonstration or staff development program, could be channeled into efforts at more systemic changes in policy and practice.

38. Employ Patience and Perseverance for Peace

Visiting the Grand Canyon in the U.S. invariably evokes feelings of awe. Standing on the north rim, Bill Timpson noted how small the Colorado River appeared off in the distance far below. "It's mind boggling to imagine the workings of weather and water over the past two billion years combining their forces to whittle the smallest crevices into gigantic canyons, the sturdiest boulders eventually into pebbles and sand. As a peace scholar who is frequently frustrated at the slow pace of change, a visit to this canyon is a helpful reminder about the importance of patience and perseverance in sustaining the peace movement, that small and personal contributions in different communities across the planet will, in time, chisel out the dark overhangs of violence and dissolve them into a free flowing and life-affirming river of peace and reconciliation."

Find photographs and descriptions of the Grand Canyon. Where do you find the patience and perseverance you need to promote peace and reconciliation?

39. Make Peace with Fears and Get Involved

Daniel Reinholz is a graduate teaching assistant who understands what it takes for students to make peace with their fears and demonstrate the kind of confidence needed to master higher-level concepts. "Focusing on positives rather than negatives can go a long way. Especially when someone is feeling nervous or uncertain, a small amount of praise or an expression of appreciation can make a huge difference. I have learned that such acknowledgments will be seen as more sincere if they are made directly. These efforts don't require much effort and can go a long way toward building personal connections. I try to model these kinds of responses and encourage students to do likewise."

Describe your own fears around learning. What subject areas are the most challenging and why? When have praise and appreciations helped you make peace with those fears? How have you helped others reconcile their struggles to learn?

Many people never encounter the needs of others in a firsthand, face-to-face, personal manner. It is easier to discuss an issue or injustice from the safety of our office, school, or home. It takes less of our valuable time to give money to a good cause. It is much safer, less invasive, and impersonal to address injustice from a distance. But when we actually take a little time to get our hands dirty in working toward a solution, or when we take a little time to make ourselves present amidst other people, we may take a big step toward understanding, justice, and love.

In *Growing Up Generous*, Roehlkepartain, et al. (1989) commented "humanizing and personalizing the issues can have an immediate, significant impact on young people" (112). Engaging youth (and adults!) in the needs of those around them will help humanize the people, the problems, and the injustice that others may encounter regularly. By humanizing the issues, the people and problems become real, and youth can personalize the issue. Make the experience tangible, unforgettable, and engaging by providing opportunities for authentic engagement between two very different people. Get involved: humanize, personalize.

40. Study the Natural World for Insights into Peacemaking

As a returning Peace Corps volunteer, Gailmarie Kimmel helped begin the Peace and Conflict Studies Program at the University of California, Berkeley. In her piece for the forthcoming book, *From Battleground to Common Ground: Stories of Conflict, Reconciliation, Renewal and Place* (Timpson, Valdez, and Giffey forthcoming), she describes her origins as a peacemaker. "As a kid, I was primarily curious about the natural world and found the adventures of Jacques Cousteau and Jane Goodall mesmerizing. Their approach taught me to see patterns in nature that allowed for beauty and balance to prevail even as food, territory, and mating meant inevitable competition and conflict, and natural forces brought occasional disasters. For as long as I can remember, I had a strong intuition that an unseen intelligence pervaded all of life and that cooperation had to be the foundation for bodies, communities, ecosystems and, yes, the best of human endeavor. I was particularly struck by the intricate communication systems of ants and bees, and found it only natural to mimic such successes in work ethic and a taste for the sweeter things in life. So I guess I was inclined toward peacemaking by being born a naturalist."

Analyze your own roots as a peacemaker. What inspiration can you draw from the natural world as a learner? As a teacher?

PEACE BUILDING

It is one thing to separate warring parties and re-establish peace. It is another thing to support peacemaking and develop the skills with communication, negotiation, mediation, and cooperation. It is yet another thing to engage in peace building that develops deep cultural commitments to peace and tolerance. Peace building at the macro level involves the development of human and institutional capacities (Whaley and Piazza-Georgi 1997) to create a "positive" peace—a process and condition where social, political, and economic structures foster the conditions necessary to eliminate both direct and indirect forms of violence. Peace building at the micro level fosters attitudes, values, behaviors, and social structures that support cohesion and authentic harmony within communities and social institutions.

41. Build Empathy for Intercultural Peace: Use Position-Taking Introductions

Deep listening and position-taking through an empathetic process are crucial for improving relationships that foster a positive environment. In the context of intercultural communication, empathy is understood as "…the imaginative, intellectual, and emotional participation in another person's experience" (Bennett 1979, 418). Through self-to-other dialogic interactions and position-taking, one can participate, both intellectually and emotionally, in the experience of the "other." By doing so, one begins to understand the existence of multiple perspectives and emotions experienced in a diverse world. Complexity and the relativism of different viewpoints and emotions might emerge from such position-taking (Brantmeier 2008). Typically, at the beginning of a group meeting, individuals introduce themselves. Position-taking is a different icebreaking approach that promotes intercultural empathy for peace— a theme to be touched upon again and again in peacemaking and peace building work.

In a group, ask people to pick a partner they do not know. Give them a script or collectively generate a script of typical and atypical questions: educational background; hometown/state/country; favorite childhood memory; something extraordinary about the person; experience of "diversity"; most outlandish wish, etc. Have them interview one another, writing down their partner's response. During oral introductions, have the interviewer stand in the foreground and the interviewee in the background. The interviewer speaks from the first person perspective, as if he or she were the person interviewed. Have both people introduce each other from this first person perspective. Ask: How did it feel to speak as if you were someone else? How did it feel to be represented by someone else? What did you learn from this process?

42. Eat Together and Celebrate Common Ground for Peaceful Coexistence

A Denver based non-profit group, Common Tables, believes that peaceful coexistence among people can emerge when they get to know each other better. Their strategy is simple: use common meals to offer people a starting point for finding greater understanding, tolerance, and appreciation. They bring people together from diverse faiths, backgrounds, and cultures in an attempt to overcome barriers, misconceptions, and fear-based thinking about those things that make them different.

From its web site, the organizers of Common Tables write, "Each of us can think differently about diversity and inclusion by recognizing one important truth: we have much more in common than we do in difference. Common Tables members are making great friends while satisfying their yearning for learning, growing, and great food. In a short time, these small group interactions will generate the momentum needed for respect and understanding to circle the world" (see: www.commontables.org). Meredith Laine, an experienced college instructor of business, says, "I read about this in *The Healing Path* (March/April, 2008). Our local communities and neighborhoods could benefit from organizing small groups like these. By starting where we live, we can begin to learn to understand our cultural differences and become more of a global family."

Reflect on experiences you have had when "breaking bread together" helped you connect with people different from yourself. Organize a dinner or potluck and invite people from different faith groups, cultures, social classes, age groups, or areas of your community. Have some questions or prompts in mind to stimulate sharing of experiences of crossing boundaries and developing new appreciations.

43. Cultivate a Sense of Universal Responsibility for Building Peace

The Dalai Lama (1999) writes about a peace building ethic, universal responsibility: "To develop a sense of universal responsibility—of the universal dimension of our every act and of the equal right of all others to happiness and not to suffer—is to develop an attitude of mind where when we see an opportunity to benefit others, we will take it in preference to merely looking after our narrow interests" (162-163).

Other-centeredness rather than self-centeredness emerges as a powerful force when cultivating the peace building self. Peace builders are those who actively seek out opportunities to benefit others—sometimes at the expense of self-interest or self-aggrandizement. Sometimes other-centered action results in mutually beneficial outcomes for all people or parties involved.

Create action inventories of recent acts under the following three categories: self-interested acts, other-centered acts, and mutually beneficial acts. Invite individuals into small groups to talk about their action inventories. Ask the groups to pick one from each category (self, other, and mutually beneficial acts) and create a skit that exemplifies those scenarios. Ask them to perform the skits for other groups. Then ask those in the audience the following questions: Reflect on the actions and outcomes within the skit.

- Who benefitted from the actions?
- Who did not?
- How was power wielded?
- Were positive or negative emotions present?
- Were positive or negative outcomes present?
- How might the scenario be changed for the better of all?

As a debriefing exercise, ask the acting groups which scenarios felt right or better and why?

44. Prevent Violence and Build Capacity for Peace

In an editorial for the *International Herald Tribune,* South African Bishop Desmond Tutu (2008) argued for both proactive intervention and prevention "when a government is unwilling or unable to stop mass atrocities being committed within its borders." He writes:

The Universal Declaration was adopted in the aftermath of World War II, the Holocaust, and the use of nuclear weapons. World opinion came together then to say, "never again." Yet in the past six decades, we have witnessed mass atrocities committed against others across the globe. We all share a responsibility to do whatever we can to help prevent and protect one another from such violence. The place to start is with prevention: through measures aimed in particular at building state capacity, remedying grievances, and ensuring the rule of law. My hope is that in the future, the *Responsibility to Protect* will be exercised not after the murder and rape of innocent people, but when community tensions and political unrest begin. It is by preventing, rather than reacting, that we can truly fulfill our shared responsibility to end the worst forms of human rights abuses.

Describe a conflict that has impacted your school, organization, family, or community. What prevention efforts and "capacity building" would have made a positive difference?

45. Create Hands of Heroes and Share Ideas for a Peaceful Future

Rooted in connectivity and creativity, the activity Hands of Heroes allows people an opportunity to share honestly about the pain that they see in their world, as well as the ideas that they have for peaceful futures. For this activity, you will need paper and writing utensils for everyone. Younger people may want a variety of colors or markers, pens, or pencils. After distributing the materials, explain that there are really no set requirements in this activity other than to allow people an opportunity to reflect on themselves and their communities as well as provide a place to dream about things that they long for in their world.

Begin by tracing your hands on the sheet of paper. Then draw or write things in your hands-spaces that are items of non-peace or violence. Think of some examples. You can use words or pictures to represent hate, anger, and violence, or you may have specific stories from your own life and community that you want to put into the hand. Allow for a period of silence for this.

After people have completed this part of the activity, you can ask yourself or others: What did you feel while you were filling in your hand? What types of things did you write down or draw? Understand that no one has an obligation to share but everyone is welcome to.

After this, look outside the tracing of your hand. Here people can write or draw things that represent peace to them. These might be words such as love, balance, and community, or they may be specific aspects of family members or personal experiences. This can also be a place to write down dreams that they have for their own lives, communities, or the world. An example might be, a dream that someday war will not be an option for solving conflict. Allow for some time for participants to complete this. You can also invite a conversation about what participants included by using the earlier questions or some of your own.

When people have completed their hands, ask them to put their hand back over what they had originally traced. Discuss the significance of this gesture, that covers all items of non-peace, and that their hands are surrounded only by peaceful dreams, words, and experiences. If people are comfortable, you may take some time to have them cover another participant hand and read about the dreams of that individual. This is a good time to acknowledge the role that we have in working together. If there is an area where these hands can be displayed, encourage everyone to explore possibilities for greater sharing, for example, covering each others hands and seeing other visions of a peaceful future.

When asked about a source for this activity, Cassandra Poncelow had this to say: "I don't have a source for it. I've used it a lot with youth groups and ministry teams over the years and it is something that was developed out of several different activities that I rolled into one. It has been a really powerful experience for students and I just modified it to focus more on the peace element, versus a prayer practice that I traditionally use."

46. Master the Basics of Peacemaking

In *Concepts and Choices for Teaching,* Bill Timpson and Sue Doe (2008) make the case for *mastery learning,* especially when there are specific skills and information to be modeled, learned, practiced, assessed, and refined. "*Mastery learning* is an instructional model promoted widely by John Carroll (1963), Benjamin Bloom (1973), and others to ensure a foundation for learning and build student self-confidence by concentrating on concise segments of the curriculum and objective feedback. Founded on the principle that students should demonstrate competence at one level before moving on to the next, mastery learning rests on a foundation of faith in student ability to learn, indeed that nearly all will learn, *if* we provide sufficient time, adequate materials and appropriate instruction. When we organize instruction in this way, the consistent success which students experience can build confidence and enthusiasm for further learning. While much of Bloom's original work focused on students in inner city schools, the concepts that emerged are especially applicable whenever students need an academic foundation (e.g., for reading or math), a specific set of skills (e.g., laboratory equipment or computer), or wherever they enter with different backgrounds, aptitude, and motivation. Much good research supports mastery learning and many college and university instructors have adopted various aspects of this approach" (175).

For anyone interested in peace and reconciliation studies, mastery represents a rich repository of research and practice for focusing on those essential skills of listening, empathic expressing, consensus building, negotiating, conflict management, etc. Seek out sources on mastery learning and think about the skills that you think are essential. What specific goals and objectives (i.e., observable behaviors) would you set? Where and how could you see these skills modeled? Practiced? What assessments would be useful?

For example, Stephanie King notes the role of language for defining peace and its varied components.

Recently, a local pastor preached a sermon about peace. Just as I was preparing to hear another message about the evils of war and another call for people to love thy enemy, the pastor redefined peace in a way that changed my perceptions. Using the Hebrew word *shalom,* which is often simply translated as *peace*, the pastor explained the fullness of the meaning of *shalom. Shalom* does not only mean freedom from war, conflict, and discord, rather, a hope for *shalom* embodies the hope for all good things that God intended for people.

The pastor told us that *Shalom* is often used as a greeting or a way to wish someone well-being. A wish or prayer for *shalom* means that you are wishing a person completeness, soundness, good welfare, health, and prosperity. This is peace. If a *shalom*-like peace embraces all the good things God intends for humans, then peace is ensuring no one goes hungry; then peace is ensuring each child has the opportunity for an education; then peace is ensuring that everyone has access to good healthcare; then peace is ensuring each person has a place to lay their head at night; then peace is striving toward greater justice for all. So, how can I help ensure *shalom* for others in this world?

Stephanie then offers an idea any of us can master: "Next time you greet an old friend or a new acquaintance, a coworker, or a stranger, greet them with *Shalom* or some other culture's word for peace. Wishing a person all the good things they could need is the first step in actively working toward peace for all people."

47. Create Learning Communities for Peace and Reconciliation

In *The Keys to Effective Schools,* Judith Warren Little (2007) describes what schools can do to support ongoing improvement and high performance. Creating "professional learning communities" clearly helps staff collaborate, support, and assist each other. What has proven effective for schools can work in any organization that wants to develop a greater capacity to address conflict management and reconcile differences.

Overall, the prospects for school improvement grow as schools take deliberate steps to reduce the isolation of teachers and to build professional communication that is both intensive and extensive. Along the path from isolation to community are several possibilities worth cultivating: steady support for individual explorations, reason, and opportunity for small collaborations, and a school-wide environment conducive to teacher learning. (56)

Assess your own organizations, groups, and networks for their abilities to support ongoing learning about peace and reconciliation for their staff and members. Ask the following questions: How could people be better connected and their isolation reduced? How could communication be improved in both quality and reach? How could individuals and small groups be better supported for exploring new possibilities? What would enhance a commitment to ongoing improvement?

48. Develop "True Dialogue" for Deeper Communication and Greater Caring

In *Teaching Diversity,* Mona Schatz (2003) describes her fears and flight from one campus when her involvement in a Holocaust awareness effort made her a target for stalking and harassment by a low-level university staff member. As she emerged from a self-imposed silence on social issues at another university, she wrote about the communication model she developed to promote a deeper communication. "When engaged in true dialogue, the main objective is to move toward greater understanding and the sharing of meaning. Dialogue does not seek out any tangible outcome. Most importantly, ideas, beliefs, and attitudes are not seen as inherently right or wrong. Dialogue groups are used to create a sense of community and wholeness. Bohm and Nichol (1996) and others (Krishnamurti and Bohm 1986) believe that if a process is created that leads to the development of true understanding of meaning, people will be transformed. The processes of dialogue groups can move members away from competitive ways of being in social interactions and toward more egalitarian and caring relationships" (127), the kind of foundation we need for greater peace and more reconciliation.

Schatz goes on to lay out some basic principles for what she terms "True Dialogue." "(1) Contract for and establish an atmosphere of trust, respect, and safety. (2) Model what you expect. (3) Use varied learning approaches, particularly approaches that enhance student participation, as well as their ability to express difficult opinions, ideas, and questions. (4) Promote student abilities to support other class members, validating and respectfully questioning each other. (5) When a class has been discussing a sensitive topic, watch the time so that there can be a 5-10 minute closure process. This allows the teacher/facilitator to tie together what has occurred" (128).

Examine your own life for examples of "true dialogue." What experiences approached, matched, or exceeded what Schatz describes? What would happen if you brought these five principles into your next class or meeting?

49. Develop Deep Listening as a Peacemaking Skill

In *Teaching and Learning Peace,* Bill Timpson (2002) makes a case for teaching deep or reflective listening as a foundational peacemaking skill. Drawing on the popularity of classics like Steven Covey's (1989) *The Seven Habits of Highly Effective People* and Tom Gordon's (1974) *Teacher Effectiveness Training,* certain basic listening principles can be established and practiced: e.g., seek first to understand, help clarify thoughts and feelings, minimize questioning, and keep your opinions on hold.

In his first year Honors Peacemaking seminar, Timpson will break students up into pairs and give them a topic like, "Assess Yourself as a Peacemaker." First one student will be the speaker for three minutes, and then the other. After each has a turn, they will compare assessments, rating the person listening on a five-point scale from #1 as low to #5 as high. During the debriefing process other issues often emerge; e.g., the role of nonverbal communication or gestures, body language, facial expressions, and eye contact. Students easily understand that this is a special kind of listening, for example, when there is a conflict and someone needs help in sorting out the issues, emotions and next steps. These skills then become some of the building blocks for more effective group work.

50. Learn to Express Empathically

Empathy is a powerful mechanism for building relationships, especially when there has been conflict. It can work for individuals, in groups, and across national borders. Our communication skills can help build peace and reconcile differences. In *Teacher Effectiveness Training,* Tom Gordon (1974) notes how effective "I-messages" can be for defusing confrontations, lowering defensiveness, and encouraging open, honest dialogue:

1. (Description) "When you..."

2. (Emotional statement) "I feel . . ."

3. (Explanation) "because . . ."

This rather formulaic model avoids judgment and emphasizes the sharing of heart-felt reactions with reasons.

In *Teaching and Learning Peace,* Bill Timpson (2002) extends this standard model to include three additional steps:

1. (Empathize) "I can imagine that you are feeling . . ."

2. (Expression of a positive) "However, I know that in the past you have been able to . . ."

3. (Clear behavioral request) "Can we meet soon to discuss this further and reach an agreement?"

As an example, when asked for a demonstration of how this model works in his first year Honors Peacemaking seminar during Fall 2008 during the run-up to the U.S. elections, Timpson provided an example of how he would use an empathic expression with each candidate for president. For Senator John McCain:

1. (Description): "When you were videotaped singing 'Bomb Bomb Bomb Bomb Bomb Iran' to the Beach Boys tune of 'Bar Bar Bar Bar Barbara Ann.'"

2. (Feeling Statement): "I was very upset . . ."

3. (Explanation): "because a leader of your stature should know how others will react."

4. (Empathize): "I know that you were joking."

5. (Expression of a positive): "And I also know that you have been a model of calm during other crises like the Wall Street meltdown."

6. (Clear behavioral request): "My request to you is that you apologize for that "joke" and be more reserved about off-handed comments in the future."

For candidate Barack Obama, Timpson came up with this example:

1. (Description): "When you have stated your intent to cross the borders of sovereign nations to kill Bin Laden."

2. (Feeling Statement): "I was shocked . . ."

3. (Explanation): "because our rule of law has always been sacred to me and hunting him down to kill him would lower us to a level of vigilante justice."

4. (Empathize): "I know that you wanted to make a very strong statement about your intent to defend the U.S. and bring its enemies to justice."

5. (Expression of a positive): "But I also know that you were opposed to the Iraq War from the very beginning and have been very public in your concern for the loss of life that followed that invasion."

6. (Clear behavioral request): "My request to you is that you affirm your commitment to the rule of law in the U.S., and that every person is due a 'day in court.' That is what we provided the Nazi leaders after World War II ended. That is what we should provide Bin Laden if we capture him."

Practice these steps with your own conflicts. Note what is easy and what is more difficult.

51. Use Consensus to Fully Explore Alternatives

For teachers at all levels, consensus is a well-established mechanism for encouraging deeper listening and empathic understanding (Gordon 1974). What works at the classroom level, however, has meaning for governments as well. While voting has long been considered essential to a democratic process, it is a commitment to consensus, where everyone agrees, that forces a group to take the time to understand the range of opinion among their members and explore alternative solutions.

For example, after the Japanese attacks on Pearl Harbor, the U.S. Congress was quick to unite in response to President Roosevelt's call to arms. After the September 11th attacks on the World Trade Center and the Pentagon in 2001, many in the U.S. were united in wanting to strike back. While the U.S. Congress was quick to endorse the Patriot Act, we later learned later that buried in the fine print were dangerous infringements on the liberties of U.S. citizens. In 2003 we saw near consensus in Congress in support of President George W. Bush's call for an invasion of Iraq, using the fear of "weapons of mass destruction" being built up in that country. Later, those few dissenting votes took on greater significance when we learned that there were no weapons of mass destruction, when the war went badly and that the "intelligence" data had been "spun." The power of consensus comes through its demand that the majority slows its rush to judgment and listens more deeply to the concerns of the minority.

Typically the consensus process begins with *problem definition* and then moves to *brainstorming,* where judgment is withheld. Once a full range of ideas has surfaced, only then does the process move to an *exploration of the consequences* of various ideas and a *group decision.* However, the consensus process does not end here; it goes further and requires an *assessment* of the decision and, if needed, some *adjustments.*

Analyze your own experiences with voting and consensus. What has worked for each, what has not, and why? How important were the skills of deep or reflective listening? Empathy and understanding?

52. Investigate Programs that Further Peace and Reconciliation

In their work on teaching sustainability, Timpson and his colleagues make a compelling argument for local activism, for applying lessons learned in the classroom with possibilities on campus and in the surrounding community and region. "Many valuable resources are available through libraries, organizations, and web sites. Help students and others develop skills for focusing their investigations, searching through resources, and identifying sustainable solutions. For example, with its emphasis on promoting sustainability in higher education, Second Nature has developed a treasure chest of materials for teaching, curriculum, institutional policy, and more . . . Assign local projects to students that draw on these ideas" (2006, 87).

As with work toward sustainability, peace and reconciliation require long-term consideration of "people, profits, and the planet." Investigate what is happening on other campuses and in other communities. In Fort Collins, Colorado, for example, there is an active restorative justice program at the university and in the city. "Dances of Universal Peace" has been meeting weekly near campus for those who want to mix movement and song with inspiring texts from various faith and cultural traditions. With a delicate voice, a sure command of her guitar and an infectious smile, Grace Marie leads. Drawing on sacred texts and prayers from various faiths—Christian, Jewish, Sufi, Buddhist, Native American, African American gospel, and more—she teaches simple songs and dance movements, and then leads a group through several rounds before ending in a prayer-like moment of silence. Much like a square dance, participants get to "dance" with everyone, holding hands or linking arms and making eye contact while singing messages about love, acceptance, peace, harmony, and respect for the Earth. Newcomers to the dances often feel somewhat anxious about this degree of contact and intimacy with strangers, but their fears usually evaporate quickly as they are swept up into an active, engaging, meaningful, and fun practice of those deeper qualities most of us say we value.

"Peace Circles" are also used in the schools to step outside the formal curriculum and create spaces for open, heartfelt exploration of more personal issues. Note the enthusiasm in the testimony from Mallorie Bruns who began working with peace circles while still a high school student. Since then she has helped bring this process to both the university and larger community. For the book, *Battleground to Common Ground: Stories of Conflict, Reconciliation, Renewal and Place,* she wrote the following: "I have seen miraculous things happen in circle, including forgiveness of others and understandings reached that I never thought possible. I trust the circle process and I know that peace will prevail in the future; it is up to all of us to decide the scale to which it will exist. I do what I can and that is all that can be done. I dream of one day sharing this peaceful program with the international community based on the work that I have done here in my own backyard. If *Peace Circle* can work to restore my community, I know it can heal many others in its own unique way."

Explore ways to start your own versions of these or other programs in your class, school, group, organization, or area.

53. Create Soldiers of Peace and Reconciliation

In *No Future Without Forgiveness,* Bishop Desmond Tutu (1999) describes the reconciliation process adopted in South Africa to begin healing the wounds left from years of a brutal, racist policy of apartheid that kept the black majority under the iron fist of the government's security forces. On both sides of the racial divide, certain stories emerged that help explain why the country was able to avoid the bloodshed that most people predicted would occur, and instead move peacefully toward democratic control.

Tutu writes, "Chris Hani, who was later assassinated on the eve of our historic elections (in 1994), had established his unassailable place in the hearts of the militant township youth. . . A military man himself, he could have drawn hordes to his side had he declared himself opposed to the negotiation process, if he had aligned himself to those who wanted to continue the armed struggle. Instead he took his reputation in his hands and went around the country urging the youth to be henceforth 'soldiers of peace,' and the youth responded enthusiastically to the call to work for peace and reconciliation" (42).

When have you seen others resist the call to arms and instead advocate for peace? How do we recruit veterans with military experiences to be "soldiers for peace and reconciliation"?

54. Build Something out of the Ashes of Violence

Claire McGlynn is a peace education scholar at Queen's University in Belfast, Northern Ireland. She writes: "In the fall of 2008 I was busy taking a workshop on Diversity and Inclusion with a new group of Catholic and Protestant student teachers. This is demanding, because it involves discussion of issues relating to religion, politics, and identity that are usually avoided because of their divisive nature. As the students began their first activity, I received a text message to say that my local Gaelic games club (a predominantly Catholic organization committed to sustaining Gaelic sports and culture) had been destroyed by fire. Instinctively I knew that this was not accidental and by the time I returned home that night and inspected the damage for myself it was abundantly clear that this was an arson attack, most likely in retaliation for the daubing of IRA (Irish Republican Army) graffiti on a local Orange Order (Protestant) meeting hall. It was terribly sad to see a recently refurbished community centre in ashes, along with many historical artefacts including photographs of the team with whom my son won the championship. There was a palpable sense of disbelief and fear, not least because people had finally been starting to accept that the 'bad old days' were over. There was also a sense of relief that no one had been hurt.

"I was struck by the tentative nature of peace and how easily sectarian sentiments could be aroused and mobilized in such a way. It was hard to reconcile this hurtful act of vandalism with the hopes that my students expressed for the future. However, out of the ashes of this fire came a number of positive aspects. Firstly, the response to the club from right across Northern Ireland was strongly supportive, denouncing violence and providing strong leadership in all quarters to resist further acts of retaliation. Secondly, the Gaelic club renewed its efforts to be more inclusive of all members of the local community, redoubling its attempts to reach out particularly to young Protestant people. Thirdly, there was a groundswell of support for building a new centre that is open to all, irrespective of religious background, and plans are already taking shape for a bigger and better community centre."

What can we learn about the precarious condition of peace from this story? What does it teach us about the mobilization of partisan reaction and how it can be defused? What examples of hope emerging out of violence can you share with each other?

55. Drink Three Cups of Tea for Peaceful Coexistence

In his inspiring stories about building schools in Pakistan, a part of the world which continues to roil with violence, American Greg Mortenson transformed himself from mountain climber to benefactor in return for the generosity that one small village exhibited when he was lost, delirious, and close to death after his failed assent of K2. The lessons he learned have deep meaning for anyone concerned with peace and reconciliation. "That day, Haji Ali taught me the most important lesson I've ever learned in my life," Mortenson says. "We Americans think you have to accomplish everything quickly. We're the country of thirty-minute power lunches and two-minute football drills. Our leaders thought their 'shock and awe' campaign could end the war in Iraq before it even started. Haji Ali taught me to share three cups of tea, to slow down and make building relationships as important as building projects. He taught me that I had more to learn from the people I work with than I could ever hope to teach them" (Mortenson and Pelin 2006, 150).

When have you had to slow down and invest in building an important relationship? When have you learned more than you have been able to teach? How has this affected peace and reconciliation in your life or the lives of those you touch?

Stephanie King offers a parallel thought about giving. "As a society, we in the United States often prize our stuff: nice clothes, big houses, fancy cars, and the latest technology. While some attempt to fill their lives with this stuff in the hopes of being fulfilled, others find much greater benefit from de-materializing and simplifying their lives. Not only can this remove the clutter from life, but it can also provide an opportunity to develop personal, internal peace.

"In *The Quiltmaker's Gift*, the quiltmaker teaches the king that true happiness would not be found in his stuff and the lavish gifts he received, but through the joy of giving to others. One by one, he gave all of his possessions to others and finds that sense of peace or fulfillment he had been lacking. As the king says in the end, 'I may look poor, but in truth my heart is full to bursting'" (Brumbeau and de Marcken 2000).

CELEBRATING PEACE

Many schools have spirit assemblies, especially when the big game looms or recent champions are honored. Situated in one of the conflicted border areas between Catholic and Protestant communities in Belfast, Northern Ireland, however, Hazelwood Integrated College is different. It has peacemaking at the center of its school curriculum and uses school-wide assemblies to focus on historic events like the Holocaust and the lessons that must be learned for today. How can we do more to celebrate peacemaking in our communities and organizations, locally, and nationally?

56. Create Your Own Nobel Peace Prize

Have you ever considered offering your own version of the Nobel Peace Prize? We should recognize when a student, faculty, or staff member acts like a peacemaker, like someone who is committed to resolving conflicts in constructive and creative ways, restoring lost harmony and healing any hurts. We need to reinforce and highlight these kinds of positive behaviors.

Kim Watchorn, an experienced teacher who leads staff development efforts, wants to see the idea of a Nobel Peace Prize replicated on a local level. "All too often, too much attention goes to those who cause problems or conflicts—the drama kings and queens, the bullies, the cranks. However, rather than awarding people who are performing their 'jobs' in a professional manner, we could make a public acknowledgment of those special actions that honor the work of those who have stepped beyond their roles and acted with nobility in a quest for peace and reconciliation. By adding a ceremony and award, we educate others about the value we place on peacemaking, the kinds of actions we will celebrate."

57. Study and Re-Create the Symbols of Peace

Dean Nelson is a combat veteran who now refers to himself as a "peacenik." He writes: "Although different peace symbols are used throughout the world, the meanings are typically the same, that is, the absence of war, strife and suffering, a nicer and gentler world free from fear. Several symbols seem to have near universal appeal, e.g., the white dove with an olive branch. Others may be associated more with a particular culture; e.g., the peace crane. Helping people learn more about the origins of these symbols can lead to valuable discoveries and rich discussions."

For example, Nelson found that the origin of the white dove as a symbol of peace has its roots in the Bible and the story of Noah's Ark. The olive branch in its bill signaled the end of the flood and God's forgiveness. The peace crane has its origins in post World War Two Japan and the story of Sadako Sasaki and the thousand paper cranes. The following description can be found on the web site for the Children's Peace Monument in Hiroshima's Peace Memorial Park:

> Visitors to Peace Memorial Park see brightly colored paper cranes everywhere. These paper cranes come originally from the ancient Japanese tradition of origami or paper folding, but today they are known as a symbol of peace. They are folded as a wish for peace in many countries around the world. This connection between paper cranes and peace can be traced back to a young girl named Sadako Sasaki, who died of leukemia ten years after the atomic bombing.

> Sadako was two years old when she was exposed to the A-bomb. She had no apparent injuries and grew into a strong and healthy girl. However, nine years later, in the fall when she was in the sixth grade of elementary school (1954), she suddenly developed signs of an illness. In February of the following year, she was diagnosed with leukemia and was admitted to the Hiroshima Red Cross Hospital. Believing that folding paper cranes would help her recover, she kept folding them to the end, but on October 25, 1955, after an eight-month struggle with the disease, she passed away.

> Sadako's death triggered a campaign to build a monument to pray for world peace and the peaceful repose of the many children killed by the atomic bomb. The Children's Peace Monument that stands in Peace Park was built with funds donated from all over Japan. Later, this story spread to the world, and now, approximately 10 million cranes are offered each year before the Children's Peace Monument. (See http://www.city.hiroshima.jp/shimin/heiwa/crane.html)

Try your hand at folding a peace crane. Get others involved. Write wishes for peace in the paper squares. You can find directions on various web sites including some that are animated: http://origami.org.uk/origamicrane.htm. You can display your cranes locally or, if you want, send them to Hiroshima's Peace Memorial Park by using the directions provided on their website.

UNDERSTANDING DIFFERENT BELIEF & FAITH SYSTEMS

As Abraham Lincoln famously asked for at his first inaugural address, when the threat of Civil War was very real, but no one could have imagined the horror of 600,000 dead, so many more wounded and scarred, and great regions of the land laid waste, "The mystic chords of memory stretching from every battlefield and patriot grave to every living heart and hearthstone, all over this broad land, will yet swell the chorus of the organ when again touched, as surely they will be by the better angels of our nature." Despite the occasional and violent antagonisms that emerge along the fault lines of competing religions, we can look for the "better angels" of peace and reconciliation that reside within each.

58. Keep the Faith about Peace and Reconciliation

When the attacks of September 11th, 2001 occurred in the U.S., Bill Timpson was scheduled to meet his large lecture class for first-year students later that morning. He had often used music as a way to transition into a particular topic. For example, he had used Bob Marley's reggae classic *One Love* as a general and optimistic introduction to his course, *College Learning for a Sustainable Future*. On this particular day, Timpson found himself wanting to say something about hope and faith in the darkest hours. He quickly went to the soulful *a cappella* by a wonderfully original African American and politically aware group called *Sweet Honey in the Rock*. Their song, *I Remember, I Believe*, chronicles a faith that helped them and so many others through the hardest of times.

> I don't know how my mother walked her trouble down
> I don't know how my father stood his ground
> I don't know how my people survived slavery
> I do remember, that's why I believe

I don't know why the rivers overflow their banks
I don't know why the snow falls and covers the ground
I don't know why the hurricane sweeps thru the land now and then
Standing in the rain, I believe

I don't know why the angels woke me up this morning soon
I don't know why the blood still runs through my veins
I don't know how I rate to run another day
I am here still running, I believe

My God calls to me in the morning dew
The power of the universe knows my name
Gave me a song to sing and sent me on my way
I raise my voice for justice, I believe (Reagon 1995)

In the midst of conflict, what music speaks to your hopes? When you need to reconcile differences, what sustains your faith? What "angels" help you wake up to meet another day?

59. Utilize Contemplative Practices in Counseling and Education

Achieving a sustainable peace and some reconciliation for old wounds means much more than the cessation of violence. It demands serious study. For example, those studying to become counselors and teachers are in need of understanding their own world views and cultural perspectives, as well as those of their clients and students. Spiritual and religious beliefs and practices are important aspects of this cultural perspective taking. In a course developed at Colorado State University, Nathalie Kees creates an environment where counselors and teachers can experience a variety of contemplative practices from many of the major world religions and spiritual traditions.

The experiential nature of this course is helpful in two ways. Students are able to experience, in a non-threatening way, some of the beliefs and practices of religious and spiritual traditions that may be very different from their own. Secondly, students can choose to incorporate various practices into their own lives and professions in whichever ways seem appropriate. Examples might include: practicing mindfulness meditation as a way of staying centered and present focused when working with clients or students, individually or in groups. Experiencing mindfulness meditations such as Buddhist Tonglen, Hindu Yoga Nidra, and Christian Centering Prayer, helps students see the universality of some of the practices and beliefs of major world religions. Mental health practitioners and teachers from various spiritual traditions serve as guest presenters and allow students to ask questions in a safe and non-judgmental atmosphere. Transferring new awareness and understanding to their personal and professional lives is done through discussions, papers, and projects; drawing upon literature in the fields of counseling, teaching, religion, and spirituality.

60. Emulate Some Quaker Peace Practices

As a practicing Quaker, counseling student, and life coach, Maggie Graham describes several Quaker peace practices that can be adapted for both individual and group use. Quakers have over 300 years of history in advancing peace, and the structures that this faith community has developed give respect to individuals' views, provide a forum for free expression of those views (even when those views may be unpopular), and build in space for deep reflection.

One mechanism for fostering reflection is the Quaker testimony. Rather than follow a specific creed, Quakers follow the idea of God (other words that are often used here include *Inner Light* and *divine*) in each person, with the expression of that spirit varying across individuals. Quakers (also known as Friends) have a peace testimony, but it is not a written epistle as the name suggests. Rather, it is the suggestion that individuals seek guidance within and follow those inner leadings.

> On the simplest level, "testimony" means "bearing witness" and the Friends' long heritage of witnessing to peace can be found in public statements and personal reflections, in their refusal to bear arms in times of civil and international conflict, in acts of prophetic confrontation and of quiet, reconciling diplomacy. But these are merely outward and visible signs of inward conviction. This conviction springs from a living Spirit, mediated through the human experience of those trying to understand and follow its leadings. (Leavitt 2004) (See http://www.pym.org/publish/pamphlets/peace.htm)

One fruitful exercise is to develop a personal peace testimony by writing down your own beliefs regarding peace. Use your personal peace testimony to guide your actions, and reflect daily on whether you follow your own beliefs and your own inner leadings. What would you write in your personal peace testimony? When your personal actions stray from your beliefs, gently guide yourself back to your own convictions.

Quakers also have a practice of posing queries to themselves or within a group. Queries are open-ended questions that invite deep reflection. They provide a structure for examining our own core beliefs, and because Quakerism has such strong roots in peace activism, many queries have already been posed in Quaker writings. Examples include:

- How do I nourish peace within myself as I work for peace in the world?
- What are we doing to remove the causes of war and destruction of the planet, and to bring about lasting peace?
- Do we reach out to all parties in a conflict with courage and love? (http://www.quaker.org/pacific-ym/fp/pymfp2001pg042.html)

If you developed your own queries, what would they say? Who would you like to ask to consider your queries?

Quakers often gather in a forum called *worship sharing* where they address queries aloud. They take turns speaking from silence to share their personal reflections on pre-arranged queries. The forum cultivates respectful listening rather than a dialog or discussion, with silence punctuating each person's sharing, so that both speaker and listener may absorb and integrate what has been spoken.

If you were to host your own worship sharing, whom would you invite? What would be your agenda in arranging a worship sharing? How would you preserve the spirit of the gathering and encourage deep listening?

61. Create a Clearness Committee

Have you struggled with a personal decision that impacts peace and reconciliation, e.g., your role as an activist on local issues or as a mediator in resolving a conflict at work? When people grapple with an intensely personal decision, finding their way to clarity often goes beyond speaking to friends, journaling or mulling over the issues as they see them. As committed pacifists, Quakers/Friends developed clearness committees to aid members of Quaker meetings in making personal decisions. Life coach Maggie Graham describes how these practices can be used.

"Within the Quaker community, the process for forming a clearness committee is triggered when a Friend with a personal concern approaches his or her Meeting (the equivalent of a church, synagogue, or mosque in many other faiths) with a request for a clearness committee. A committee of three to five people is appointed, and logistical arrangements are made for the committee's first (and sometimes only) meeting.

"The clearness committee begins with a statement from the requestor, either verbally at the start of the meeting, or in writing prior to the meeting. Silence punctuates each person's contributions to the meeting, with the substance of the speaking centered on open-ended questions addressed to the requestor. The tone of the clearness committee meeting is one of deeper reflection and support for the person at the center of the committee. The requestor drives the meeting either with responses to the questions or with spoken reflection. Generally, a clearness committee meets for two to three hours at one sitting, and it may reconvene over the course of several weeks or months as the requestor seeks further clarity.

"The purpose of the committee is to provide the requestor with the space and time to examine the issues facing him or her in a supportive environment. Questions are posed by committee members without an agenda, often following intuition and leadings. Giving advice is forbidden, and the contents of the sacred forum are generally not discussed beyond the structure of the committee meetings. The meeting is held solely in support of the person at its center."

If you were to request a clearness committee, what would you want to discuss about your contributions to peace and reconciliation? Whom would you invite? To structure it according to Quaker practice, consult Parker Palmer's *The Courage to Teach* (1998).

Quaker practices offer many other structures that can be easily adapted for individual and group use. Information about the Quaker faith and practice can be found at http://www.quaker.org/pacific-ym/fp/index.html.

UNDERSTANDING CONFLICT & RESTORATIVE PRACTICES

There is much to draw on to criticize traditional approaches to justice. With high recidivism rates, the likelihood that those already in jail will, after release, return to jail raises serious questions about our notions of prison rehabilitation. In the U.S., high rates of incarceration generally, and of minority males in particular, underscore wasted lives and lost opportunities. For example, while U.S. prisons overflow with those convicted of drug use, other nations have chosen to treat addiction as a medical problem and use their health professionals. What we learn from Maori and the institutionalization of restorative justice in New Zealand is the value of an emphasis on learning and the restoration of harmony so that those who have committed crimes or hurt others admit to their errors, ask for forgiveness, learn from the victim and others how their actions caused harm, and then agree to some form of community service to repair the damage done. We can see similar processes at work in South Africa as that country emerged from years of violence, in part, through the activities of the Truth and Reconciliation Commission and its exchange of amnesty for truth telling about wrong doing. In essence, the nation learned about the horrific toll of a state-imposed apartheid as victims and families on both sides of the political divide had an opportunity to tell their stories and hear a plea for forgiveness from their tormentors. Lessons of violence were translated into processes of reconciliation so that the nation could move forward toward a peaceful and inclusive future. We see similar processes among some Native American groups in the United States.

62. Shift from Retributive to Restorative Justice as a Means of Reconciliation

In *No Future without Forgiveness*, Bishop Desmond Tutu (1999) describes how his native country of South Africa used the Truth and Reconciliation Trials to shift away from a legalistic pursuit of justice and punishment as was evident during the Nuremberg Trials of Nazi leaders after World War II. Instead, amnesty was offered to many of those who had committed the crimes of apartheid in South Africa, a system of state control and terror that was used to suppress the majority black population, as well as those crimes that were committed in retaliation by various guerilla factions.

In practice, this meant a trade off of justice for healing, reparations, and education as perpetrators came forward to tell openly of their crimes without the mediation of courts, lawyers, judges, the rules of law, and arguments about guilt or innocence. The entire nation of South Africa heard directly from those who committed these atrocities and how the government had condoned, ordered, or provoked these crimes.

Tutu writes about extending these lessons learned about forgiveness to other nations: "A year after the genocide of 1994 in Rwanda, when at least half a million people were massacred, I visited that blighted land. . . . I told them that the cycle of reprisal and counter reprisal that had characterized their national history had to be broken and that the only way to do that was to go beyond retributive justice to restorative justice, to move on to forgiveness, because without it there was no future" (257, 260).

Revisit what we know about the Abu Ghraib prison scandal during the U.S. led war in Iraq. Research and list the "punishments" that were meted out to those military personnel who were convicted. Now brainstorm what would be different if a "restorative model" had been followed and the focus shifted to healing, reparations, and education.

63. Forgive and Honor Memories

Reconciliation can be difficult, especially when the wounds are deep. Forgiving acts of violence can be especially challenging, for individuals, groups, and nations. Andrea Taylor has had much to reconcile and forgive. She is an experienced teacher, school leader and innovator, professional artist, a great grandmother, and a doctoral student when she wrote this: *"Happy families are all alike; every unhappy family is unhappy in its own way.'* This opening line from Tolstoy's *Anna Karenina* has come back to me many times since I first read it years ago. As a child, I longed for the security and nurturing that I thought my friends had—whether they actually did or not. Both my parents were alcoholic and ended up divorcing when I was 10: my mom moved away and my dad married one woman after another, trying to find someone to raise me and my little sister, I think. I witnessed domestic violence, felt the pain of abandonment, and experienced loss that no child should have to. I literally cried myself through childhood. Both parents died young in today's standards. But before they did, I came to terms with my pain by facing what their choices had done to my early life and simply forgave them.

"The one thing I remember (and I have so few *real* memories of my early years with my mother) was that when we were little she made us Jell-O®. Not just any Jell-O®, though; it was lime Jell-O® with whipped cream, crushed pine-apple, and walnuts. When my children were young, in an act of honoring her, I made it for them. It has developed into a family tradition now and my children are making it for theirs. Such a small thing—Jell-O®. Such a big thing—forgive-ness."

Identify those simple acts and experiences that you associate with some-one you need to forgive. Practice, teach and model that forgiveness to others.

64. Imagine Possibilities and Act

Violence can destroy possibilities and cripple the spirit. Yet, somehow, people do survive, finding hope and inspiration in different places, their creativity rekindled. Andrea Taylor has learned many lessons from a childhood that left her too often traumatized. In particular, she has found so many new and positive experiences through an exploration of creative outlets. "I like to remember the line from George Elliot, 'It is never too late to be what you might have been.' As an injured or neglected person progresses through Maslow's (1959) hierarchy of human needs, something begins to happen; unexpected things, wonderful things. Von Oech (1986) talks about the four roles involved in the creative process—explorer, artist, judge, and warrior—and it is at the point of Maslow's highest stage of "self-actualization" that they can spontaneously appear.

"For me, it was the artist. I began to imagine possibilities and to act on them. I had not sensed any creativity in me during my turbulent childhood, into adolescence, or well in to my adult life. Then one day it happened. I began to paint—simple, focused watercolor. This demonstration of deep heart-healing has brought about a wonderful new dimension to my life. I have met new friends. I have ventured out into new territory—hanging my paintings in public places, selling them to people across the country! As a teacher, I believe that what I do must reach further than the thing just done. It is my hope that I can reach those students who need my help to become who 'they might have been'!"

When has creative exploration helped you move past old hurts and seen new possibilities? When have you helped others take those first steps?

65. Restore Hope and Instill Motivation

Conflicts can traumatize the strongest of spirits. Yet, somehow people can also learn the lessons that help define their character. Andrea Taylor learned about hope and motivation by surviving some very tough circumstances. She vividly remembers the time when she was stopped short by something she had seen in a novel by Marilyn French: "You don't have to shoot a woman to kill her; all you have to do—is marry her." When I read this line many years ago, I dropped my head into my hands and wept—right there in front of everyone. That is what it felt like to me. After an emotionally blighted childhood, I found myself pregnant at sixteen, then married, and later abandoned with three little ones to raise on my own. For many, that might be the end, but not for me.

"With a deep desire for something more, I pressed through the natural tendencies to give up, and just let life happen. I passed the test and received a GED, relocated to a college town and found a job on campus. After 17 years of working and going to school, I earned a BA in English with teaching credentials. Within a few months of graduating from college, I remarried and relocated to the Seattle area with a new and blended family. Within two years, I was working with street kids in Seattle's inner city in a junior and senior high school that I founded. The kids in our school desperately needed that deep desire that I had felt many years ago. It became our stated mission *to restore hope* to their hearts and *instill motivation* to their minds so that they, too, could press through and find another kind of life. The school is now in its 19th year."

Make a list of those experiences that have helped restore hope for you. Who has helped motivate you to "press through" tough times and leave something of lasting value?

66. Help Restore Happiness and Create Fulfilling Lives

As Nel Noddings (2003) suggests in her book, *Happiness and Education*, at the present time educators and those interested in education are focusing on financial aims in schools—educating students to support a strong economy and to be financially successful, rather than to flourish as adults. We need to remember the key to what helps us to flourish is living happy, peaceful, and fulfilling lives. Tom Cavanagh writes: "I suggest if we want our children to be happy and flourish as adults, then we need to ask them what makes them happy and help them learn how to build healthy relationships and heal broken relationships."

Using the Peacemaking Circle process (with a talking stick), let us take the time to ask the students we teach what makes them happy and listen to their answers.

67. Understand Indigenous Conceptions of Caring

The idea of caring is closely associated with peace and reconciliation. Nel Noddings is well known for her work regarding how teachers can create a caring environment in their classrooms. Tom Cavanagh has studied restorative practices in New Zealand and found a fascinating variation of this culture of care. "An indigenous colleague helped me understand caring from an indigenous perspective. This respected Maori scholar told me two Maori words describe this deeper understanding of caring—*manaakitanga* and *mana motuhake*. In this context, I understand *manaakitanga* to mean the responsibility of the host to care for the well being of the visitor, that is, to entertain, to look after, and to offer an invitation to the visitor to experience hospitality. *Mana motuhake* was a phrase used by Maori political activists in the 1980s to combine the words relating to power and independence into a phrase meaning self-determination or autonomy."

Clearly the idea of teacher as "host" has a very different connotation than teacher as task-master, disciplinarian, or standard bearer. The question we can ask is how other Maori cultural understandings of caring can help deepen our conceptualization of how we create peaceful, caring relationships in classrooms. You can learn more about these ideas by reading Bishop and Berryman's book, *Culture Speaks: Cultural Relationships and Classroom Learning* (2006).

68. Promote Restorative Justice and Violence Reduction

Many of us talk about peace education and restorative justice, but not everyone practices it daily as Wendy Cohen does. The life of Wendy Cohen's daughter Lacy was taken in a violent murder in 2003, when Lacy was 21 and working toward her teaching license at the University of Northern Colorado. Since that time, Wendy has spent her energy and resources forging an incredible journey of restorative justice and violence reduction in honor of the life of her daughter.

One of Wendy's first acts of restorative justice was when she asked the court to consider life imprisonment for her daughter's killer instead of the death penalty. As they left court that day, Wendy reached out to the mother of Lacy's killer and hugged her, realizing that both mothers had lost a child. Wendy and James Clausen, the brother of Lacy's killer, have spent the past several years speaking together publicly about the experiences and losses of the family of the victim and the perpetrator. No one is left unaffected by acts of violence, or by their presentations.

Wendy has also created 2 Hearts: The Lacy Jo Miller Foundation and a school called 2 Hearts Academy. The students in her school are often referred from the juvenile justice system or have not been successful in the public schools for a variety of reasons. The curriculum for the school has been developed out of Wendy's 20+ years as a teacher of high-risk children. It focuses on violence reduction and restorative justice through providing knowledge and information, expanding students' choices, improving self-esteem and decision making skills, and providing service to the school and community. Creating a safe and nurturing environment where students feel respected and welcomed is at the foundation of the school's success.

Have participants read some of the other offerings at the www.2Hearts 4Lacy.org website. Follow up with a discussion related to the following questions. How would you have reacted if you were Wendy? How would you have reacted if you were the brother, sister, mother, or father of Lacy's killer? What role can community service play in violence reduction and restorative justice?

69. Practice Ifoga and Promote Reconciliation

In Samoan culture the answer to dispute healing (rather than resolution) is *ifoga*. *Ifoga* is a ceremony in which an apology in the *faasamoa* or Samoan way is offered. This ceremony involves the village rather than an individual. This apology is offered to the person harmed and to their family or village. Considered to be an act of reconciliation, *ifoga* literally means an act of bowing down. The purpose of *ifoga* is to avoid retribution and to maintain peace (Tuala-Warren 2002).

While engaging in *ifoga* is only appropriate in Samoan culture, as Western people we can learn from this powerful Samoan ritual. First of all, apology is an important part of reconciliation. Secondly, the harm caused by disputes or conflicts affects the whole village or community, not just an individual.

Western educators might well ask themselves: do we make space for people to offer apology to the people harmed, and do we think broadly about the ripple effect of harm? When we respond to disputes or conflicts by avoidance, elimination, or asking an expert to solve the problem, we remove the opportunity for apology and reconciliation. How can we respond to disputes and conflicts in a way that allows for and encourages apology?

70. Establish Truth and Reconciliation Commissions

In *No Future Without Forgiveness*, South African Bishop Desmond Tutu (1999) describes the process by which those who had committed "political crimes" or had acted "under orders" from a superior, typically within the police or other state security apparatus, could apply for amnesty from prosecution if they told the truth and asked for forgiveness. Above all, Tutu, Mandela, and other leaders wanted to educate the nation and the world about the horrors of apartheid. Establishing the Truth and Reconciliation Commission was the mechanism.

Tutu writes about one case: "Five police officers, in amnesty applications that detailed the killings of dozens of people from the Pretoria region, described how they had tortured their 'terrorist' quarry and how they had then disposed of the bodies. . . . You are devastated by the fact that it could be possible at all for human beings to shoot and kill a fellow human being, burn his body on a pyre, and while this cremation is going on actually enjoy a barbecue on the side. What had happened to their humanity that they could do this? . . . In many cases in the Eastern Cape, people vanished without a trace as a result of their bodies being burned to ashes. . . . Nevertheless the full story of the killing, . . . and in particular the identities of the killers, emerged only when the commission was set up" (126, 130).

What historical events in your lifetime would benefit from something like a public "Truth and Reconciliation Commission" hearing? How can "state terror," in particular—e.g., police riots, torture, illegal covert actions—as occurred in South Africa be made public and new preventative policies enacted? What events in the life of your school, college or organization could benefit from greater openness and transparency?

71. Remember the Past and Do Something to Promote Reconciliation

Archbishop Desmond Tutu (1999) reports on the Truth and Reconciliation Commission that he chaired as South Africa tried to heal from the ravages of apartheid. He describes the difficult and tortuous path that the commission tried to walk in addressing the horrors of the past with honesty, reparations, and sensitivity, while simultaneously hoping that forgiveness would be possible as a foundation for an inclusive future.

Tutu writes: "Many white people in South Africa have come to see themselves as entitled to reconciliation and forgiveness without their having to lift so much as a little finger to aid this crucial and demanding process. This is a broad generalization, which in the way of generalizations does not do justice to those whites who have been outstanding in their commitment to justice and who were in the thick of things in the dark days of apartheid's awful repression. Many of those in this distinguished group had to run the gauntlet of the hostility of their white community. They faced ostracism and frequently had to suffer the sort of harassment and vilification, and sometimes detention and torture, that were the lot of those who dared to stand up to be counted, who were willing to swim against the current in a country where all this was anathema. Their contribution was incalculable and indispensable, and I want to pay them all a very richly deserved and warm tribute. Having said that, I have sadly to note that a very large section of the white community have forgotten, far too easily and far too soon, that our country was indeed on the verge of catastrophe which could have seen us overwhelmed by the kind of carnage and unrest that have characterized places such as Bosnia, Kosovo, the Middle East, and Northern Ireland" (164).

What historical events or periods can you identify where the majority population was "too quick" to forget its role in repression and too neglectful of the sacrifices that had to be made? For example, many Americans, both white and black, seem to have forgotten how Martin Luther King Jr., now mythologized as an iconic champion of Civil Rights and nonviolence, was vilified for taking the fight for integration into the North, for extending the movement to include poor people, and for coming out against the war in Vietnam. Yet, at the same time, King was considered "safer" than other more militant blacks like Malcolm X, Stokely Carmichael, and the Black Panthers. What historical events in your school, university, or organization should be revisited because too many are too quick to forget problems that may still require attention?

72. Maintain Positive and Peaceful Relationships

Larry Brendtro (2006) tells us that students that cause educators the most trouble are often "kids in pain." Bullies often mask their insecurities with aggression and violence. He has based his work on the extensive research of James Anglin (2003). What Brendtro says is that these "kids in pain" suffer from "deep and pervasive psycho-emotional pain." As a result they have developed counterproductive and self-defeating behaviors. Our tendency as educators is to react to these behaviors by inflicting even more pain into their lives as punishment in the hopes it will stop the offending behavior. However, this reaction feeds an emotional reaction (ER) cycle that is pain-based and ineffective. Zero tolerance policies are typical of this approach to discipline.

Brendtro suggests that the effective way to respond to the misbehavior of these "kids in pain" is by "developing and maintaining positive relationships." By using the power of empathy and building the capacity (resilience) of these young people, educators can create restorative changes in them and begin to heal their long-standing wounds. To paraphrase Archbishop Desmond Tutu: We must look on children in need as potential sources of important information, if given the opportunity to tell us.

Stephanie King offers this improbable but sweet story as a reminder of what is possible when disaster strikes and the needs are great. "It is easy and comforting to spend time with familiar company. Reaching out of our comfort zones to encounter new and different people can be scary and can take such great effort. Yet, opening to new possibilities by making friends with people with whom we generally would not spend time can broaden our horizons, teach us about other people and ourselves, and bring new sources of peace and love into our lives.

"In *Owen and Mzee* (Hatkoff, Hatkoff, and Kahumbu 2006), we can read the amazing but true story of a 130-year old giant tortoise (Mzee) who cares for a baby hippopotamus (Owen). After Owen is separated from his family during a tsunami, he and Mzee find themselves together in captivity where they develop a most unlikely friendship. Before meeting Owen, Mzee seemed content to live alone, maintaining almost an antisocial existence. Baby Owen, however, needed a mother to care for him. While no one would have expected these two creatures to bond so deeply, each found something necessary in the other."

Ask yourself: How can I develop a positive relationship with a student who obviously is a "kid in pain"? How can I make peace and reconcile with anyone in pain? What has been your own experience with others when you were "in pain"?

73. Reconcile and Restore

Bill Timpson likes to keep his skills sharp for teaching about peace and reconciliation by volunteering with the Restorative Justice Program in his hometown of Fort Collins, Colorado. At monthly "Restore" sessions on Saturday mornings, first time offenders can elect to have their police record for shoplifting exonerated if they admit their guilt, join a Restorative Justice circle with peers, parents, and members of the community, and complete some agreed upon community service activities intended to help "restore" the damage done. The data for this program tell a remarkable story of the power of learning over punishment, of an emphasis on reconciliation. While U.S. recidivism rates for those in jail typically mean that over 60% of prisoners return to prison, of those who elect to participate in the Fort Collins' "Restore" Program only 2% are ever arrested for shoplifting again.

And the lessons learned? For one, many learn that "wants" and "needs" are very different; these kids may want some new stylish outfit or the latest CD, but in the circle of restorative justice they learn that these are very different from what they really need. We often talk about the pressures of a materialistic culture that equates self-worth and possessions. For another lesson, many also learn that there is usually a ripple effect for their actions, that family and friends are impacted by their selfish acts. Having a parent in the circle can begin the process of rebuilding trust. We talk about the developmental shift that happens when young people begin to mature out of their preoccupation with themselves. The lessons for peace and reconciliation are clear: (1) open and honest communication is essential; (2) where judgment and punishment can be crippling, learning can be liberating; (3) where trust has been broken, honest self-assessment and a desire to change course can begin to repair the harm caused and rebuild relationships.

Look into restorative justice programs in your own community. If none exists, look into starting one. Contact your local police or court officials to see if there is interest. Or find other volunteer opportunities where you can use these skills of listening, acceptance, collective support, and care.

When teaching her graduate classes, Ellyn Dickmann likes to address any simmering conflicts among her students through the use of "tension tables." She writes: "This activity provides a supportive and safe classroom environment to address tensions between students. Oftentimes tensions emerge as a result of cultural, political, or social differences and/or misunderstandings.

Below is an example that outlines the 4 key steps of how I utilized Tension Tables in a graduate level leadership development course.

"Step One—Introduce the Concept: At the start of the semester I introduced the concept of Tension Tables as a way to create a safe listening opportunity and a time for understanding. I reinforced that addressing tensions is necessary for healthy debates to emerge and also provides an opportunity to enhance learning.

"Step Two—Observe and Reflect: During the second and third weeks of the semester I began to observe a division in the classroom between students from the "education world" and "business and industry world." I took time outside of class to reflect on where the conflict was and created a list of potential reasons. There was frequent use of dismissive body language and comments passed back and forth between the worlds as leadership theories and concepts were presented and discussed. In addition, the class had created "camps" with the "education world" on one side of the room and the "business and industry world" on the other.

"Step Three—Set Up Tables: During the fourth week of class I started the class by sharing my observations of the class tensions and created 3 tables that had representatives from both worlds. I created three different sets of questions (one set for each table) that explored the topics of tension. A critical component of setting these tables up was allowing enough class time for in-depth conversation and sharing. In this case I allowed a full hour for the discussions and reporting out.

"Step Four—Reporting Out of Discussions: I rotated from table to table during the hour of discussions and added to the dialogue when necessary. At the end of the hour, I asked each table to report out on what they learned as well as how it felt to talk about the areas of tension that the questions addressed. As each table reported out I made comments and discussed openly how I viewed this activity as a strategy to discuss future areas of tension.

"Overall the students found the Tension Table strategy to be helpful and asked for these opportunities as the semester progressed."

Experiment with this and other ways to model constructive and creative management of conflicts among your students. You will need time, but the benefits may prove worthwhile in the long run.

74. Differentiate between Wants and Needs

Conflict erupts most often between groups of people because one or both feel they have critical and long-lasting needs that have been overlooked and because they somehow perceive the "other group" as the obstacle that has prevented those needs from being fulfilled. The need for validation of one's humanity, for equitable access to resources and opportunity, and for voice and choice are at the root of enduring conflict and violence in many nations and communities throughout the world. Teaching peace should thus include creating safe spaces where such needs and wants can be shared and clarified, without judgment.

Elavie Ndura is a peace scholar who survived the genocide in the Great Lakes Region of Africa. She writes: "In my multicultural education classes, I engage my students in an intimate discussion of their wants and needs in a culminating session after discussions of race and racism, religious diversity, gender and sexism, social class and economic equity, and the social impacts of widespread intolerance and inequity. I use the following discussion prompt: 'As a member of a particular race or ethnicity, what do you want members of other races or ethnic groups to do in order for you to prosper in this multicultural world?' I further instruct my students to 'Please control your emotions and listen without interrupting.'

"As the students take turns voicing their needs and wants, a powerful silence fills their shared space where truth is uncovered in its full authenticity, unchallenged, uninterpreted, a transformative moment for all participants. The session closes with the participants taking turns, again in deep silence, sharing the messages that they have heard, and how these messages will shape their future attitudes and behaviors in relation to people from different racial and ethnic groups."

75. Challenge the Language of Conflict

When she was a doctoral student reading Deborah Tannen's (1998) *The Argument Culture*, Stephanie Moyers wondered if the language of "doctoral defense" establishes a potentially unhealthy and unnecessarily adversarial expectation between student and committee. She also wondered if there was some connection between the fear of the defense that many students report and the numbers of ABD (All But Dissertation) students who seem to have stopped short of completion. "As I get closer to writing my dissertation, the idea of having to participate in a defense feels really intimidating because of my perception of the culture of critique being central to the process. According to my reading of McKeachie and Svinicki (2006), I know that fear can be a barrier to discussions because students are often uncertain of the response they will receive from professors and peers, or they are afraid of being embarrassed. When this happens, the safe learning environment can be destroyed and work will need to be done to rebuild the respect and trust necessary for students to feel success" (Palmer 1998; Kees 2003).

Moyers continues: "I agree with Tannen (1998) that we need to move from debate to dialogue and find creative ways to express disagreements. Would it be possible to creatively change the label of dissertation defense to something that creates a more peaceful space than one that is characterized by animosity before the student even begins to present his or her research? Would it be considered less academic if it is not labeled a dissertation defense? In class, we wondered if it would help to re-label the traditional 'defense' as 'presentation, critique, and evaluation?' Or if 'mock' or practice presentations would help de-escalate anxieties."

Examine the language that describes your work or study for evidence of presumed conflict. You could also explore other possibilities that emphasize dialogue, listening, and empathy.

76. Find Peace in Every Patch of Natural Area

Kellee Timpson has written a very personal essay for the book, *From Battleground to Common Ground: Stories of Conflict, Reconciliation, and Place.*

"Wherever I have lived, when I am out walking my dog, I am bound to stumble across walking trails, greenways, and pocket parks tucked into the neighborhood. These green spaces are easily overlooked when driving by and, even if noticed, seem too small to be significant, let alone worth driving any distance to visit. Walking my dog is my excuse to spend time outdoors and, even in these small natural areas, I usually feel more relaxed, no matter what kind of day it has been. My point is that it doesn't have to be Yosemite or the Grand Canyon. Left to itself, even the smallest patches of 'wild' hums along and goes about the natural business of living. The trees and shrubs do their best to hide the signs of urban, built environments, especially in the wilds of western Washington. And here, away from cars whizzing by, I enjoy a quiet moment watching water cascade over rocks, birds flit from tree to tree, and insects buzz from flower to shrub. Here, I feel satisfied with a renewed sense of place and purpose among the grasses, trees, and birds" (Timpson, Valdez, and Giffey forthcoming).

Identify natural areas near where you live and work. Over a period of time, remind yourself to visit each and find something "inspiring"—a tree or bush, a leaf, the grass, a rock formation or a patch of dirt, birds, insects, or the sky above. Make it a peaceful, even a meditative moment. Remember to focus on your breathing.

77. Take the Third Side

In *The Third Side*, Bill Ury (1999) describes what it means to take a proactive role in a dispute, a role that has its own risks but significant potential benefits as well. Indeed, the risks of inaction, of doing nothing, are often tragic. "The *third side* implies a new responsibility. . . . We may not think of ourselves as third parties; indeed, we generally don't. Yet, each of us has the opportunity to help stop destructive fights around us. We constitute the family, the friends, the colleagues, the neighbors, the onlookers, the witnesses. Even when no third party is present, each of us can choose to mediate our own disputes by taking the third side" (23).

Ury continues, but with some cautions: "Taking the third side is not an easy responsibility. It consumes time and energy. Those who step into the middle can find themselves criticized by one party or both for 'interfering' or 'meddling.' In potentially violent situations, thirdsiders may even run the risk of physical harm. As fighting, however, jeopardizes the happiness of our families, the productivity of our workplace, and the safety of our communities, it is increasingly in our own self-interest to act as thirdsiders. We are all stakeholders in the conflicts around us. In short, the third side is not some mysterious or special other. The third side is us—each of us acting individually and all of us working together. When it comes to stopping fights, the missing key is in our hands" (24).

Analyze the conflicts you have seen up close. What "third side" role did you or someone else play? What role could you or others have played?

SEEING INTERCONNECTIONS

At the heart of ecology is the interconnectedness of all life. In keeping with this reality is the value of systems thinking when addressing the human role in sustainability, when appreciating the benefits of diversity and inter-cultural dialogue, when seeing global relationships, and when promoting peace education and efforts toward reconciliation.

78. Multiculturalism as a Perspective on Human Life

Cultural clashes are often cited as the reason for conflicts, war, and vio-lence. Yet efforts at cross-cultural understanding are not always welcomed. For example, multiculturalism as a political doctrine has been heavily criticized and yet it would appear that human beings are deeply embedded in cultural groups that help to define us and to shape our development. What is the rationale then for inter-cultural engagement rather than peaceful co-existence and tolerance? Bhikhu Parekh (2006), a British philosopher, argues that, irrespective of its rich-ness, no single culture can embody all that is valuable in human life, nor develop the full range of human possibilities: "Different cultures thus correct and com-plement each other, expand each other's horizon of thought, and alert each other to new forms of human fulfillment" (167).

Intercultural encounters provide a space for cultural interrogation, the challenging of assumptions, conscious or unconscious borrowing of customs and behavior, and the widening of horizons, precipitating both small and large changes in those individuals involved. For Parekh, multiculturalism is not a po-litical doctrine but rather a perspective on human life that recognizes multiple ways of living the "good life." Toleration is insufficient—instead he advocates critical engagement between cultural groups that allows for the exchange of al-ternative perspectives and for dialogue that is mutually enriching.

Individually or in small groups, research one of the following questions: (1) What theoretical rationales (other than peaceful co-existence and tolerance) might inform engagement between human beings from different cultural/reli-gious/political perspectives? (2) To what extent can a concept such as multiculturalism be reworked as a theoretical tool for building peace? (3) List the necessary conditions for critical engagement between members of different cultural groups and justify your choices.

79. Understand Critical Multiculturalism as a Response to Cultural Diversity

The sources of conflict may be quite varied but violence and war often explode from a mix of economic, cultural, and ideological factors. The management of cultural diversity in education challenges our views on individual and collective rights. Critical multicultural education theory proposes that an acknowledgment of diversity divorced from a serious questioning of social inequality is fraudulent and potentially harmful. A critical multicultural perspective also questions the role of teachers and schooling in perpetuating dominant values and common culture. Critical theorists maintain that liberal forms of multiculturalism supporting belief in a natural equality and a common humanity are flawed (Kincheloe & Steinberg 1997). They argue that if commonalities are stressed rather than differences, the promotion of cultural invisibility will fail to address issues of bias. Liberal multiculturalists counter this by claiming that positive ideals such as liberty and equality need to be endorsed. They contend that such a liberal standpoint gives hope for the stable coexistence of people with diverse values.

Prepare separate arguments to support both the critical and the liberal theorists. Draw on your own experience of educational institutions to predict the possible outcomes of both perspectives. Now use your theoretical imagination to devise a perspective that might reflect the most positive elements of both positions. What challenges might your new perspective face in practice?

80. Unpack White Privilege: The Inner Circle

Peggy McIntosh's (1989) article on white privilege is nearly a classic for studying this construct, an invisible system that grants unearned privileges to whites, creates oppressive conditions for non-whites, and often leads to violence in various forms. Peace, in the context of diversity, cannot be attained through a false unity or false harmony. Rather, deep inner work needs to be done on the part of whites in order to unravel the white dominance paradigm and move from honesty to empathy, to advocacy, and to social action toward change (Howard 2006).

After reading Peggy McIntosh's (1989) article, gather with others into a tight, shoulder to shoulder circle in a large, open space. If most, or all, of the group are Anglo, ask certain participants to "position-take" with a person who is Native American, African American, Latino/a, and Asian American, i.e., speak as if that person of color. Be sure to have an ample representation of non-white people. Ask everyone to hold a sign with that label and to respond from that position. Give everyone the option to not represent her/his own race. All others will answer as white people. Read all twenty or so statements about white privilege from Peggy McIntosh's article. Those who can answer "yes" stay in the inner circle. If "no," they take one large step backward.

After all statements are read, reflect on the process and the formation. How did it feel on the outer circle? Inner circle? Position-taking with another race? What other thoughts surfaced during the process? Whose voice was heard? Whose voice was lost? How does this reflect the larger society? How can we move toward authentic racial equality and equity? Toward intercultural peace?

81. Challenge the Essentialization of Identity

Conflicts and war often push people toward simpler categorizations so that their prejudices and hatreds can be more easily enflamed by over-generalizations and propaganda. Amartya Sen (2006) argues that the presumption that people can be uniquely categorized based on their religion or culture is inaccurate. Moreover, it actually constitutes a major source of conflict in the contemporary world. Challenging such categorization is, however, tricky, not least because human beings actively seek affirmation of a positive identity, particularly in times of conflict.

We could interpret Sen's work as counter to much educational practice that celebrates religious and cultural diversity. However, rather than a wholesale rejection of multicultural practices, Sen rejects only a monocultural approach that might err by overemphasizing the homogeneity of various groups. Instead he favors a form of multicultural practice that endows the freedom to cultivate reasoned choice of identity priorities. As such, Sen distinguishes between these two approaches to multiculturalism: "one which concentrates on the promotion of diversity as a value in itself; the other approach focuses on the freedom of reasoning and decision-making, and celebrates cultural diversity to the extent that it is as freely chosen as possible by the persons involved" (150).

Much contemporary educational practice promotes the active celebration of diversity. What are the implications of Sen's arguments for the way in which you approach cultural and religious diversity in the classroom? How can you balance the human need for positive identity, the need to respect cultural and religious backgrounds, and the need to develop autonomous choice? What would the world look like if we no longer categorized people by religion and culture and what would the subsequent implications be for peace? Rethink how you introduce yourself to others: what roles do you emphasize? For many of us in the U.S., we are our work or career roles, i.e., teacher, professor, or student in this or that major and thinking about this or that career. What would change if you introduced yourself by other qualities, e.g., where you live, what your relationships are to others in your group, what you are enjoying about that particular moment or day?

82. Understand Identity and Conflict

In her award-winning book, *Education and Conflict: Complexity and Chaos,* Lyn Davies (2004) warns that attempts to preserve distinct cultures can present communities as homogenous and fixed, rather than dynamic and emerging. She argues that education can resist confirming essentialist identities that, in turn, can be mobilized for conflict in two ways: first, by acknowledging the complexity and hybridity within a person, and second, by avoiding stereotyped portrayals of the "other." In addition, in their description of the goals of peace education in intractable conflicts, Ian Harris and Mary Lee Morrison (2004) contend that educators need not only to promote respect and acceptance but also to develop a caring disposition toward members of other groups.

We can use the "Identity Iceberg" activity to explore our conceptions of identity. We know that the main part of an iceberg is actually submerged and invisible to our eye. This is the same with our identity. Above the waterline are the aspects of our identity that we wish people to see and recognize. Below the waterline are those aspects that we prefer not to be readily visible. Draw a large iceberg that fills a page and create a waterline that allows just the tip of the iceberg to be above water. Now decide where you wish to place on your iceberg the various aspects of identity (race, gender, religion, culture, socio-economic background, class, disability, ability, musical taste, clothing, etc). Place those aspects that people are usually most happy to reflect above the waterline and those that people are less happy to reflect below the waterline. Now discuss why certain aspects are placed above or below and in particular consider those aspects right at the bottom of your icebergs. Consider how this diagram might change depending on the company that you are in and then use this discussion to explore the multiplicity of identity aspects that make up a human being. How can this kind of exercise be used to challenge stereotypical reductions? In a group where trust has been established you may choose to construct personal (rather than generic) identity icebergs and then invite members of the group to share these with each other.

83. Promote an Anti-Bias (ABC) Approach

During the worst of the recent conflict in Northern Ireland, a common perception among educators was that schools should be "oases of calm" from societal violence and that, in particular, issues of religion, identity, and politics should be avoided. By contrast, the integrated school sector, which was started in 1981 by a parent pressure group who wished to see Catholic and Protestant children educated together (rather than the traditional separate provision), advocated a more upfront approach to these topics. Emerging from more than twenty five years experience in the integrated schools sector is a curriculum approach that explicitly tackles these sensitive topics head-on and is unashamedly anti-bias with regards to culture, religion, ethnicity, social background, gender, sexual orientation, and disability.

A recent handbook, *ABC: Promoting an Anti-bias Approach to Education in Northern Ireland* (pdf copy available at www.nicie.org), outlines the approach recommended. Such an approach may involve challenging previously unquestioned practices and behaviors and may meet with resistance from students, teachers, parents, support staff, administrators, and politicians. However, positive action is required in order to challenge bias. The Northern Ireland Council for Integrated Education (2008) identifies a number of characteristics that are important for engaging in anti-bias work, namely:

- a willingness to develop a positive self-identity;
- an open-mindedness and awareness of one's own bias, behavior, motivation, and limitation;
- an understanding of issues of gender, sexual orientation, ethnicity, culture, religion, class, physical and learning ability, and how these interact;
- a readiness to incorporate an anti-bias approach throughout the school community.

Consider the types of anti-bias approaches with which you are familiar. How do they compare with the Northern Ireland examples and what are their strengths and limitations? Explore the implications of an anti-bias approach for policies and practices, experiences and activities, language used with students and teachers, and for the physical environment of the classroom and its surroundings. What role can anti-bias work play in peace and reconciliation education?

84. Use a Prejudice Awareness Exercise

As part of a national effort at reconciliation, the Northern Ireland Council for Integrated Education (www.nicie.org) and the Corrymeela Community (www.corrymeela.org) have both been involved for many years in community relations training in Northern Ireland. A joint initiative between the two organizations has resulted in the production of a very useful, practical manual for schools, entitled *Joined Up: Developing Good Relations in the School Community* (Lynagh, Nichola, and Mary Potter 2005). This useful resource aims to support schools in building good relations throughout the school community as well as active learning approaches to controversial issues.

Peace education scholar Claire McGlynn writes: "One activity from this resource that I have found very useful, in particular, in my work with teacher candidates, is an activity called *Not Up My Street* which was devised by John Doherty to explore how prejudice is part of life and to reflect on how we make generalizations that can lead to prejudices being formed. The activity unfolds as follows: The whole group is told that a house in their street has become vacant and the local council has decided to consult with the residents on who should be allocated the house, as there are eight prospective tenants. The eight candidates are as follows:

- A reformed drug dealer
- An employed youth
- A retired bank manager
- A member of the Orange Order (a Protestant organization)
- A gay nurse
- A head teacher
- A Sinn Fein councillor (a Catholic/nationalist politician)
- A refugee from Eastern Europe

"Based on the above, people are invited to rank from one to eight the person they feel should be given the house. In small groups (five to six) ask them to come up with a group ranking. This may take some time depending on the negotiations and compromises necessary. Each group then feeds back its choices, along with a justification for their choice, and these are noted on a flipchart. Crucially, each group is then provided with a paragraph of further information on each candidate, material that challenges their perceptions. For example, the retired bank manager is female and took early retirement due to her involvement in fraud; the member of the Orange Order is 74 years of age and wishes to be closer to his son; the head teacher has been accused of assault by a pupil, and the refugee has a complex personal biography that might suggest suspicious activity in his home country. The groups are then asked to reconsider their rankings and these are noted on the flipchart.

"I find that this activity provides plentiful opportunity to explore assumptions, how we make decisions based on prior knowledge or perceptions, the various criteria that people use to make their selections (e.g., self-serving or altruistic), how we make judgments, how and why we label people, and how we can maintain certain prejudices and reject others."

How could you modify this activity for your own context? What kind of people would you include as prospective tenants and what information could you provide to challenge your students' perceptions of them?

85. Work towards Deconstructing Identity in Conflict and Post-Conflict Societies

From a substantial body of research in multicultural schools in three countries that have variously suffered from conflict—namely Israel, Northern Ireland, and Cyprus—peace education scholars have noted the dissimilar ways in which educators and children pay attention to identity issues as these arise in interactional encounters (Bekerman, Zembylas, and McGlynn 2008; Bekerman, Zembylas, and McGlynn forthcoming 2009). Claire McGlynn writes: "In both their rhetoric and practice, we have observed that educators tend to essentialize ethnic identity and to mark events related to these categories. The children, however, pay less attention in their social activities, although they are knowledgeable of the categories and appear to construct social worlds with less emphasis on ethnic difference. Regardless of the differences in identity found in the educational policies of Israel (emphasis on Zionist ethos), Northern Ireland (focus on pluralism) and Cyprus (emphasis on Greek-centered education), we have observed that in practice children have different perspectives. This observation provides *openings* in the system for engaging in subversive work that is grounded in children's perspectives and not in an adult's agendas.

"From our perspective, a relevant forward direction implies a radical change in educators' perspectives and their educational activity. The individual mind can no longer be the goal of these activities. Instead, we ought to consider and analyze the interactional practices and strategies through which all involved in the contextual activities allow identity or culture to make its appearance. We first need some criteria which can be accepted by all and that are 'objective' but do not rest on the positivist underpinnings of objectivism. Such criteria could be achieved through an educational process directed at questioning: Who in our societal context are exploited? Who are powerful and who powerless? Which cultural patterns carry symbolic power (Hames-García 2000)? Who are labeled as '*other*'? Who defines the norms and categories?

"We want to emphasize the importance of problematizing the identity boundaries that are created, thus opening minds to the potential of collaboration, rather than individuation. We also want to highlight concoction as the true secret of human and humane work (culture), as opposed to the establishment and maintenance of policed and institutionalized borders which serve in the preservation of that which is considered normal" (7).

Ask these questions: What implications would such an approach have for policy and practice in the educational institutions with which you are familiar? What are the implications for teacher education? How might such an approach contrast with a view of education as social reproduction rather than transformation, and with whom or what position might it come into conflict? What are the resultant implications for celebrating, for example, religious or cultural festivals in schools?

86. Understand Curriculum and Transformative Citizenship

Peace and reconciliation involve many complex and interrelated factors. As opposed to seeing them as discrete areas of study and practice, connections should be seen and forged with other areas, disciplines, and movements. For example, work on diversity and sustainability issues, and on economic equity and social justice, have much in common with work on conflict management and nonviolent solutions. Citizenship education is another curriculum that can be closely allied to peace and reconciliation education with adequate staff development and planning.

In his recent article "Diversity, Group Identity, and Citizenship Education in a Global Age," the distinguished multicultural educator James Banks (2008) explores how the existence of ethnic, religious, or linguistic diversity within a political territory presents a challenge to the ideology of nation-state. He challenges liberal assimilationist conceptions of citizenship and citizenship education that reject cultural group membership in pursuit of an "umbrella" civic identity. What Banks objects to most strongly is the inference that individuals from different groups need to give up their home and community cultures and languages in order to attain inclusion and to participate fully in the national civic culture. Instead, drawing on the US Civil Rights Movement of the 1960s and 1970s, he argues that groups can help individuals actualize their rights and opportunities.

Banks outlines a typology of levels of citizenship in order to help educators conceptualize ways of assisting students to acquire deeper citizenship. The most superficial is *legal citizenship,* which applies to members of the nation-state who do not participate in the political system in any meaningful way. The next level is *minimal citizenship*, which applies to legal citizens who vote for conventional and mainstream candidates and issues. Above this is *active citizenship,* which involves action beyond voting. This may involve protests or making public speeches that support and maintain existing social and political structures. The highest level proposed by Banks is *transformative citizenship,* which involves civic actions designed to actualize values and moral principles beyond those of existing laws and conventions. Transformative citizens take action to promote social justice even when this action may violate, challenge, or dismantle existing laws, conventions, or structures.

List examples of *transformative* citizens in your community, culture, and country. What kind of citizen actions successfully challenge the status quo and what have been the long term results of such actions? To what extent can structural change also occur through other levels of citizenship, for example, *active* citizenship? Where would you place yourself in this typology and where would you aspire to be placed? What practical steps can you take to make this progress? How can all of this relate to peace-making and peace-building?

87. Comfort and Empower with a Cultural Blanket

Peace and reconciliation require participation and initiative. Those who lack confidence in themselves and shrink from fully engaging undermine the potential for group success. In a similar way, new college students, and especially those from diverse backgrounds, can undermine their chances for success if they do not "make peace" with their estrangement and reconcile their differences. Guadalupe Salazar and Rich Salas lead El Centro Student Services at Colorado State University. Over many years they have developed a range of activities to help students from diverse cultural backgrounds establish some common ground and address their concerns. For example, while working with Latino students, they have found that it is important to incorporate family into their learning. A Latino proverb insists that "la cultura cura" or "culture heals." Salazar and Salas ask: "What happens to those students who do not feel comfortable speaking out in front of others or sharing their experiences? Too often they become disengaged and shut down. The cultural blanket is one activity that can help facilitators/instructors provide a safe and comfortable space for students who may lack the speaking skills or confidence to speak in front of a group."

"The exercise consists of providing each student an 8 inch by 8 inch piece of white cloth, markers, acrylic paints, and art supplies. For our work on campus, we may start by identifying common college experiences among these students of color or a challenge each sees. Or we may ask something about their families or personal goals. Students can either express themselves on their cloths with words or drawings, using symbols, metaphors, or proverbs. We usually allow about 45 minutes. We then ask volunteers to share something about their cloths. When everyone who wants to has spoken, we collect the cloths and sew them together in a blanket. Later, when we display our "cultural blanket," we will have a follow-up discussion about commonalities, differences, and themes."

88. Create Non-Dominating and Peaceful Relationships

Often, in talking about peace and reconciliation, the topic of diversity comes up. Use of the term "diversity" is problematic to some indigenous people because the word is closely linked with "multiculturalism" and "tolerance." These words can be interpreted as the person who belongs to the dominant culture benevolently including the person from the non-dominant culture. In seeking to build and maintain peaceful relationships we need to carefully choose the words we use and the meanings we attach to those words.

Maori scholar Professor Russell Bishop offers insight into a different way of thinking about relationships between people of different cultures. The essence of this indigenous understanding of relationships between people is brilliantly captured in this phrase coined by Professor Bishop, "non-dominating relationships between self-determining people." This Maori *whakatauki* gives further insight into this concept.

Nau te rourou, naku te rourou
Ka ora ai te iwi

With your basket and my basket
People will be nourished

A question we might ask ourselves is how can we create non-dominating relationships between self-determining people in our classrooms, organizations, and communities? You can learn more about these ideas by reading Bishop's 2005 chapter on indigenous issues about research.

89. Use Internet-Based Networks to Promote Peace and Reconciliation

Violence and war have dominated so much of the human experience over the past few centuries that too many people see aggression and bloodshed as inherent to the human experience. In the face of such assumptions, we need new thinking, new possibilities. For all that advanced technology is adapted for new and deadlier weapons, there is the parallel possibility that computers, in particular, can be used in work towards peace and reconciliation. The Internet, for example, can expand the ways in which we can connect with others from different cultures and build understanding. Social learning can help us shift from a traditional perspective (Brown and Adler 2008). People can move from simple facts to more sophisticated ideas that are essential for peace and reconciliation (Timpson 2002).

Emerging Internet applications are ideal for fostering this kind of social learning. These applications, known as Web 2.0, are dynamic and help shift the focus from static content consumption toward more content sharing and learner-to-learner interactions. As a consequence, we can help people individualize their learning and construct more socially-based understanding. Here are several hypothetical scenarios of an individualized social learning environment.

Scenario #1: A student is concerned about national security. This person knows very little about extremist groups. Realizing the complexities of these issues, the learning-facilitator (instructor) encourages this person to engage in Internet-based social learning (e.g., using tools such as Ning.com or Voice thread.com) and connect with others from around the world to construct a richer and more complete understanding of national security. This understanding may, then, expand beyond simple border protection to include global security and stabilization.

Scenario #2: Several civics instructors want to engage students in an upcoming election. The instructors establish a wiki web site (using pbworks.com or wikispaces.com) and encourage other civics teachers from around the country—or world for that matter—(via sites like www.classroom20.com) to join a conversation about the candidates and issues. People are encouraged to share their local, regional, and national perspectives. Through these discussions students will be challenged by diverse viewpoints and, we believe, better able to construct a meaningful understanding of both candidates and issues.

Scenario #3: People everywhere are concerned about global warming and what they can do to reduce their carbon footprint. Although they may feel good about their contributions, they are also aware that carbon production by emerging countries will soon eclipse the carbon savings in developed nations. In order to fully understand the social and international complexities of these issues, people can engage with others in social construction using blogger.com or WordPress.com. Using blog search sites such as Technorati.com, they can locate and follow bloggers from India and China who are writing about similar issues. Instructors can encourage students to cross-list postings with these foreign bloggers. These kinds of postings, readings, and sharing, can help students construct a more accurate awareness of the complex social nature of these issues.

90. Understand Dominance and Address the Color-blind Perspective

When teaching peace and reconciliation, it is important to fully acknowledge people's biases as they relate to racial implications. Multicultural education is a vehicle of peace and reconciliation that fosters opportunities to examine race, privilege, oppression, and dominance. For example, as part of the dominant white culture in America, there are systems of privilege at work that provide advantages to the dominant white cultural and structural group. At the same time, people of color are asked to close off their racial identity and are often excluded from the power differentials within systems of privilege that white cultural groups experience. When people from the white dominant group honestly examine the privilege and power differentials at work within their organizations, they can advocate for social justice and the greater good of humanity. But this must first start with dialogue and understanding about biases as they relate to race, racism, equality, and inequality.

The purpose of the activity described below is to introduce a discussion about how a Color-blind approach is unconsciously chosen because it can be easy to ignore someone's race. When we ignore a person's racial/ethnic background, we ignore who that person really is. The activity asks us to examine how structural aspects of racism promote inequity.

- Provide a sheet of paper that has six squares, or boxes, on it with one of the following typed in each box: Race/Ethnicity, Religion, Language, Core Values, Family, and Personal Belongings.

- Ask people to describe something about themselves in relation to these six topics. For example, describe yourself in the Race/Ethnicity box, your first language in the language box, an assessment of your honesty and respect under core values, etc.

- Give everyone the following information: Two countries are in the process of negotiating for peace. Yet, in the process of negotiations, one country still controls the other country. And the country in control has asked that the people give up one of their boxes. Ask them to cross out the box that is least important to them.

- Now ask them to talk to someone sitting nearby why he or she chose to cross out a particular box.

- Ask them to choose the next box to cross out and share that decision with their partners. Continue until there are only two boxes left.

- When only two boxes are left, compile the results for the entire group; which boxes were eliminated the most?

Teacher educator and multicultural scholar Antonette Aragon writes: "In the times that I have conducted this activity, the majority of participants often cross out race first. I'll then start a discussion about this. I'll ask participants if they agree with a Color-blind perspective and why, and record their responses on a white board or large pad of paper. I'll then show students the following quote and ask for their reactions: 'Color-blind discourse asserts that any consideration of race is itself racist. It protects racism by making it invisible' (Kandaswamy 2007, 7). I'll then try to connect this quote to their responses. This activity can also be a springboard for analyzing how race is a social construction of society and not something that is scientifically valid. Choosing to be Color-blind may promote power differentials within systems of privilege."

91. Apply the Pedagogy of Architecture

As we learn how to make and sustain peace among ourselves, to reconcile our differences in constructive and nonviolent ways, we must also learn how to make peace with the planet and reconcile our wants and needs with the carrying capacity of the earth. For example, in *Earth in Mind,* David Orr (1994) challenges us to reflect on the "lessons" that our classrooms and buildings "teach" about our values. "It is paradoxical that buildings on college and university campuses, places of intellect, characteristically show so little thought, imagination, sense of place, ecological awareness, and relation to any larger pedagogical intent. . . . My point is that the design, the construction, and the operation of academic buildings can be a liberal education in a microcosm that includes virtually every discipline in the catalog. The act of building is an opportunity to stretch the educational experience across disciplinary boundaries and across those dividing the realm of thought from that of application. It is an opportunity to work collectively on projects with practical import and to teach the art of 'good work.' It is also an opportunity to lower lifecycle costs of buildings and to reduce a large amount of unnecessary damage to the natural world incurred by careless design" (115-116). The same could be said about any renovations that are planned.

In the spirit of "making peace with the planet," ask the following: Do your students, audiences, or staff have access to natural light and fresh air? Is energy routinely wasted by leaving lights on? When being renovated, are the paints used low VOC (Volatile Organic Compound)? Is the old carpeting thrown away or recycled? Are there recycling containers readily available in rooms and hallways? Are the windows energy efficient, e.g., double pane? Is the furniture made with any reference to "green principles," e.g., locally harvested and certified wood? Instructors and group leaders can also be more creative about using field trips and outdoor spaces as "classrooms" where learning can occur within the life affirming realities of the natural world.

92. Understand How Food Connects Us Across Every Divide

In a piece for the book, *From Battleground to Common Ground: Stories of Conflict, Reconciliation, Renewal, and Place,* Jayme Winell offers the following insights: "In 2000, I lived in Bali for three months and, five years later, spent a month in China. In these two fascinating places I witnessed traditional agricultural practices and the impacts of malnutrition and starvation: small villages outside Beijing full of stick-thin children with protruding bellies, sifting through garbage; rice paddies near Ubud (Bali) submerged in water and villagers fishing in small boats for tiny, flat fish to eat. These vivid scenes were etched in my mind. Food impacts every living being. No matter what president is in office, we will still need to eat. No matter what war is ravaging whichever land, both sides will still need to eat. Sadly, food is wrapped up in politics, policy, and greed and because of this, hundreds of millions starve. In every way, food connects us across every divide" (Timpson, Valdez, and Giffey forthcoming).

In *Touching Peace,* Vietnamese Buddhist monk, Thich Nhat Hanh (1992) offered a series of mindfulness exercises that can help raise awareness of the interconnections among people that depend on peace. At your next meal or snack, for example, take some time to reflect on the food you are about to eat—i.e., the conditions under which it grew, the sun and soil and rain that nourished it, the labor that went into its harvest before you were able to receive it. Note how often hunger and starvation accompany the outbreak of war. Challenge others to bring this same mindfulness to their eating.

BUILDING A POSITIVE CLIMATE & SUPPORTING COOPERATION

Many benefits flow from efforts to create and sustain a positive and peaceful climate for any class, meeting, group, or organization (Timpson and Doe 2008). People are more willing to trust each other, to be honest and open, as well as sensitive, whenever tension surfaces and healing is needed. People are better able to address problems that arise and involve everyone affected in the decisions that are made. They have developed some sophistication about communication and are able to establish effective ground rules.

Gordon Allport's (1954) classic work, *The Nature of Prejudice,* documented the power of working together in groups to break down learned prejudices that are too often the source for violence. For example, much like the bonds that develop among members of sports teams and that cut across traditionally charged racial boundaries, individuals can quickly develop new appreciations for people they were taught to demean, dislike, or hate. The Johnson brothers, David and Roger, have documented the social and cognitive benefits of cooperative learning among school-aged youth.

93. Fall into Trust

Rebuilding and maintaining trust are essential components to peace and reconciliation processes. Fear, shame, anger, hatred, and vengeance are formidable obstacles that need to be addressed in order to promote renewal and change in conflict situations. Rope courses can promote trust, cooperation, team building, leadership, and listening skills through physical activity designed to stretch normal boundaries. (See: http://www.ropescoursesinc.com/pro grams.html.)

But you don't need a formal ropes course to demonstrate the concept. Explain that trust is essential to nurture positive relationships and to heal after conflict situations. Underscore the essential consideration for safety. Assemble groups of four to six people. Someone responsible must serve as spotter for each group. Allow for voluntary participation as "faller" and "catcher" since, for example, some people might have physical or emotional limitations. Practice clasping hands to ensure that catchers will be supportive. Be sure to discuss proper posture—catching the faller's weight with one's legs and back straight, not hunched over. Ask one person to turn her/his back to the group and the others in the group to embrace their arms in a web in order to catch the person when she or he falls backward. Ask that person to close her/his eyes, let go, and fall backward into the arms of the group. Repeat the process with all group members who are willing to participate. Reflect on some of the following questions.

What thoughts and emotions did you experience as "faller" and "catcher"? What conditions are necessary for trust? If someone declined to participate, you can ask that person to comment as well as get reactions from the group. Ask how this experience might transfer to building trust in other situations where there are conflicts between groups in society or nation-states.

94. Establish a Language for Trust

Trust can often be a difficult concept to verbalize or describe. It is not necessarily the case that trust is an ambiguous notion, but that the language used to describe it can be somewhat contextually dependent. Do you trust your partner's commitment? Do you trust the jack will hold up the car? Do you trust that the cruise control in your car will maintain a specific speed? Do you trust the actions of a group are in your best interest? Do you trust that massive military expenditures will ensure a nation security? Different contexts elicit different ideas about the nature of trust, or even what trust is not. When he was a graduate student at Colorado State University, Saun Hutchins wrote: "I personally like to identify trust with what I can expect; however, I recognize that that definition is limited to my own identification with the concept, and not entirely universal."

In efforts to measure trust, researchers have attempted to define it relative to both interpersonal relationships (Larzelere and Huston 1980) and within systems (Lee and Moray 1994; Muir and Moray 1996). Researchers were also able to provide correlational evidence that trust and distrust were in fact opposite constructs on a single continuum and not representative of differing values (Jian, Bisantz, and Drury 2000).

In order to develop scales of trust and assess identification with both trust and distrust, researchers had to compile large lists of trust representative words called semantic fields. It is these word lists that may also prove beneficial for teaching peace and reconciliation. Saun Hutchins noted, "from a strictly personal experience, I have seen that communication is a primary condition for fostering trust between both individuals and groups. A diverse and broad vocabulary for trust could be considered yet another condition for successful communication about trust."

Common Vocabulary

Table 1 provides a list of the top 15 elicited words associated with trust and distrust. There is no meaningful ordering of the presentation of the words. Jian, Bisantz, and Drury (2000) include lists of up to 30 words for each opposing concept; however, only the top 15 are shown in the example below. From the adapted word list in Table 1, we can see that trust can be identified with a variety of descriptors.

An important part of teaching peace and fostering trust may be first to establish a common vocabulary for reference, understanding, and association. Prior to displaying the results of this study, ask people who may be either in conflict with one another or neutral toward one another to create a semantic field for the words *trust* and *distrust*. Ask them to brainstorm how conditions of trust can be built and how conditions of mistrust can be transformed. Ask them to apply the semantic fields in an analysis of how to resolve and to transform a specific existing conflict.

95. Collaborate and Contribute

The more connected we are with others, the more we know them, the less likely we are to see hard lines of differences that can undermine trust. In *147 Tips for Teaching Sustainability,* Timpson et al. (2006) draw on ecological principles of interdependence and interconnection to make a case for shared responsibility and creativity in designing new projects. "Architecture students at the Ecole des Beaux Arts in nineteenth-century Paris completed short, intense problem-solving assignments. The professor wheeled a cart *(charrette)* through the studio classroom to collect the projects, as students frantically worked to complete their solutions. Today's design *charrettes,* or community design workshops, involve interdisciplinary groups—including project stake-holders—collaborating, brainstorming, and setting common goals for proposed projects such as construction of a new school, public library, housing development, or similar effort" (74-75).

In the development of *147 Tips for Teaching Peace and Reconciliation,* we enlisted contributions far and wide. In your own work and life, you could identify an existing group, committee, or task force that could be challenged to contribute something new and creative toward peace and reconciliation. Write up the results in an editorial or letter to the editor for a local newspaper and emphasize connections with the writings of the great peacemakers.

96. Be, Live, and Learn in Peaceful Relationships

As the theory of a culture of care in schools is advanced (Cavanagh, 2008), educators learn that building healthy relationships is at the core of peaceful and non-violent schools. From that foundation flow three domains: being, living, and learning in relationships. Inspired by the work of Deloria and Wildcat (2001), we know that:

TRUST	DISTRUST
Entrusting	Deceiving
Promise	Lie
Assurance	Falsehood
Security	Betrayal
Reliability	Mistrust
Fidelity	Treachery
Loyal	Cheating
Integrity	Steal
Trustworthy	Phony
Honest	Misleading
Honorable	Sneaky
Confidence	Wariness
Love	Suspicion
Friendship	Cruelty
Familiarity	Harm

Table 1: Trust and distrust terms

Being in relationships is at the core of what schools are about. Often in today's environment, curriculum has replaced relationships as the foundation of schooling. Schools can have the best curriculum, but if relationships are not healthy, they will fail.

Living in relationships means recognizing that relationships are important inside and outside of the classroom. Rather than thinking in terms of us-versus-them (e.g., teachers versus students, good students versus bad students), educators need to encourage a sense of solidarity or "all for all." In a culture of solidarity, respect for the dignity of all is critical. Creating new responses to wrongdoing and conflict in schools that do not rely on labeling students, and that separate the person from the problem, maintains dignity.

Learning in relationships focuses on classroom relationships and interactions between teachers and students, and among students, as being central to learning. Rather than maintaining a narrow focus on teaching the curriculum, teachers need to pay attention to the customs, habits, and practices in their classrooms. These processes are much more effective in informing teachers about their teaching than simply evaluating the results of standardized tests. In turn, students are made to feel welcomed and comfortable with who they are and what they bring to the classroom.

Evaluate your relationships for their potential for impacting your *being, living,* and *learning.*

97. Build and Sustain Peaceful Networks

When the twentieth century came to a close and she completed *Cultures of Peace,* Elise Boulding (2000) stepped back to reflect upon what had been and what was needed. "We are in the middle of rough times as I write, and much rougher times lie ahead. The challenge is to draw on the best of the hopes and the best of the learning skills, and the relationship-building networking, and coalition-forming skills that have developed in this past century, so that the long-term future may yet birth new cultures of peace" (257).

Assess the role of your own networks in supporting yourself through tough times. What have you learned about coalition building that has made a difference for you and others? What new "learning skills" have you had to develop? What "cultures of peace" have you created for yourself?

DEVELOPING EMOTIONAL INTELLIGENCE

Violence will always evoke the strongest of feelings—fear, terror, desperation, hatred, anger, a desire for vengeance, and/or the deepest sorrows. In his work on multiple intelligences, Howard Gardner focuses on "intrapersonal" and "interpersonal" intelligences, knowing self and knowing how to relate to others. In *Emotional Intelligence,* Dan Goleman (1994) argues that our success and happiness in life, whether at work or at home, with colleagues, friends, family, or by ourselves, has much more to do with our ability to manage our emotions and interact with others than with what our formal diplomas indicate is our expertise. Consider all those abilities that we include within peace and reconciliation. Goleman writes: "There are widespread exceptions to the rule that IQ predicts success—many (or more) exceptions than cases that fit the rule. At best, IQ contributes about 20 percent to the factors that determine life success, which leaves 80 percent to other forces. . . . My concern is with a key set of these 'other characteristics,' *emotional intelligence:* abilities such as being able to motivate oneself and persist in the face of frustrations; to control impulse and delay gratification; to regulate one's mood and keep distress from swamping the ability to think; to empathize and how" (34).

While formal schooling concentrates on knowledge and skills, so much in life depends on the ways in which we handle our own emotions internally as well as in response to others. Dan Goleman and Howard Gardner have each written extensively about "emotional intelligence," the awareness and skill that impact both our "intrapersonal" as well as our "interpersonal" lives.

98. Address Emotional Intelligence and Development

In *Teaching and Learning Peace,* Bill Timpson (2002) describes his use of scenes from particular movies to illustrate the costs of violence and to discuss alternatives. "Ever since the 1997 killings at Columbine High School, I have used a clip from the film, *Basketball Diaries,* starring Leonardo DiCaprio to illustrate how some individuals, modeling what they see in a movie, will resort to violence as a response to feeling marginalized, seeking revenge and perhaps notoriety by gunning down perceived persecutors. The 'dream sequence' in this movie shows DiCaprio, dressed in a long black leather coat, bursting into a classroom and gunning down classmates. How life can imitate art!

"Although the movie character wakes up and moves on, ultimately getting his life together, the Columbine killers chose to focus on this killing scene, making reference to it in their emails as they planned and then executed their murderous plot. While some students, and especially those with direct links to Columbine High School in Colorado, have found this clip deeply disturbing, most see it as directly relevant and useful for illustrating course concepts of emotional intelligence and cognitive development. The question remains, however: do these scenes add to an existing memory bank of violent images that only serves to desensitize or can they be memorable links to important new insights about peaceful alternatives?" (113).

In the summer of 2008, Timpson took a tour of the political murals in Belfast, Northern Ireland to hear some background explanations from a local guide for the "Troubles" and their aftermath that took the lives of so many in the 1970s, 1980s and 1990s. "Aaron" grew up Protestant but was steered clear of the violence by parents who had the moral courage to teach tolerance. When his own mother was badly injured in a bombing, however, his father decided to move toward the outskirts of Belfast even though those who left were often referred to as "shirkers." Aaron later found out who set the bomb but decided not to retaliate. He insists that he has forgiven that man.

Identify times in your own life when you decided not to retaliate. List the consequences. Compare these with times when you did retaliate. What insights do you get when you share these with others and hear their stories?

In *Teaching Diversity,* Roe Bubar and Irene Vernon (2003) describe the challenges they face as Native American lawyers and scholars when teaching about Indian history and law. "One of the great difficulties in teaching federal Indian law is coming to terms with our own legal education and the indoctrination process we ourselves endured. . . . Colonization, boarding school policies, assimilation, and relocation policies were largely glossed over, and the underlying cultural racism that is pervasive in our laws, politics, and court decisions was not addressed. When we began to teach federal Indian law, we both found it was difficult to reread certain cases because we began to experience again the anger we felt over what we did not learn. We were forced to remember all those academic conversations about a justice system that demeaned Native American beliefs and histories" (160-161).

A study of peace and reconciliation has similar challenges. There can be a general suppression of dissent, especially in times of war or when there is a drumbeat call to "support our troops." For some there may also be a kind of indoctrination into a surface patriotism that insists "my country right or wrong." Others may struggle to identify their own beliefs or find alternative views when powerful interest groups, in the private or public sectors, can influence the media and spin the "news." In the midst of these challenges there is also the requirement for "emotional intelligence," for handling anger or difficult memories of violence.

Analyze the effects of "indoctrination" on your own thinking. Read about Dan Goleman's notions of "emotional intelligence" or Howard Gardner's ideas about "multiple intelligences"—intrapersonal and interpersonal intelligence—and assess your abilities to handle anger.

99. Correct Misplaced Aggression in the Media

If journalists and reporters focus only on the tragic, the bloody, and the sensational, peacemaking and reconciliation will always suffer. In her critique of an American preoccupation with debate and competition in *The Argument Culture,* sociolinguist Deborah Tannen (1998) makes a case for pushing journalists and reporters away from the personal and toward the constructive. "Continual attacks on leaders distract both the leaders and the citizens of the nation from problems that need to be solved. According to the Pew Center survey, a whopping 65 percent of the public said that press coverage of the personal and ethical behavior of political leaders is excessive. But fewer than half thought that press criticism of the policies and proposals of political leaders is excessive. In other words, the problem is not too much aggression but misplaced aggression" (92).

Analyze press reports about political leaders over several weeks. Determine what percent of the coverage touched on the personal and the ethical and what percent touched on policies and proposals. Compare your own reactions to what was reported in this Pew Center survey as described by Tannen.

100. Transform Motivation into Constructive Change

In the video series on nonviolence for PBS, *A Force More Powerful* (2000), movements for freedom and social justice from around the world and in different historical contexts are connected to the pioneering efforts of Gandhi to introduce nonviolence as a mechanism for change. In one program, the origins of the Civil Rights Movement in the U.S. are traced to efforts at desegregation in Nashville, Tennessee. We see the African American students at Fisk University, one of the country's prominent, historically black colleges and universities (HBCU). Early scenes depict leaders in the black community holding workshops to explain how a campaign of nonviolence could confront racist power and control. Attempting to integrate a downtown lunch counter, volunteers take the abuse of whites without resorting to revenge. The media is alerted so that the attention that ensues arouses support locally and nationally. Throughout this campaign, nonviolence was framed as a courageous act and the antithesis of the weakness or inadequacy that some associate with pacifism.

The work of Rudolph Dreikurs (1968), in particular, offers a useful framework for understanding violence and rethinking responses. In his work on classroom conflicts and student misbehavior in schools, Dreikurs hypothesized that without being taught or shown how to get their needs met in positive ways, students may escalate from wanting attention to seeking power and control, and then to feeling inadequate.

Explore the value of Dreikurs' framework for other programs in the six-part PBS series on nonviolent change, *A Force More Powerful*—Chile, South Africa, India, Poland, and Denmark. Identify another film, videotape or DVD that contains examples of violence. Draw on the work of Dreikurs to analyze the behaviors of those in conflict, i.e., (1) Attention, (2) Power and Control, (3) Revenge, and (4) Helplessness and Inadequacy. Analyze the events portrayed on the screen within this framework and explore how responses could be reframed in a constructive manner that encourages peace and reconciliation.

101. Rethink Revenge

If attacked, it is easy to understand the impulse for revenge. In part, it's that hard-wired "fight or flight" response. In part, it's anger and how we manage our own emotions. In part, it's intellectual, the ideas we have about the world and when we should or should not strike back. We are obviously influenced by the role models we honor. Some of us are also affected by the practices we adopt, the meditation or prayer we use to stay grounded in our values and in control of emotions that otherwise could spin into aggression, hostility, and violence, reactions that we later come to regret, especially when we reflect on the tragic consequences and losses that are associated with war.

In his autobiography, *Long Walk to Freedom,* Nelson Mandela (1994) describes the toll that hatred and a thirst for revenge exacts on individuals and a nation. Enduring twenty-seven years in prison, Mandela could have emerged bitter and determined to exact revenge. Instead he argues for principles of a deeper liberation. "Freedom is indivisible; the chains on any one of my people were the chains on all of them, the chains on all of my people were the chains on me. It was during those long and lonely years that my hunger for the freedom of my own people became a hunger for the freedom of all people, white and black. I knew it as well as I knew anything that the oppressor must be liberated just as surely as the oppressed. A man who takes away another man's freedom is a prisoner of hatred; he is locked behind the bars of prejudice and narrow-mindedness. I am not truly free if I am taking away someone else's freedom, just as surely as I am not free when my freedom is taken away from me. The oppressed and the oppressor alike are robbed of their humanity" (624).

Examine your own experiences, when you have thirsted for revenge. Drawing on Mandela's principles of an inclusive freedom that moves past old hatreds, speculate on what would have been different for yourself and others if you could have found other, more peaceful responses.

Maurice Friedman (2000) offers an important re-interpretation of the Old Testament ethic of an "eye for an eye." Many of us have always understood that idea as a moral argument in defense of revenge and a major barrier to healing, forgiveness, and peace. In areas where groups come into conflict, it is easy to see how the combatants on both sides who adhere to this scripture could get locked into a bitter and bloody pursuit of revenge. Just who would have the last killing? As Gandhi famously said, "An eye for an eye makes the whole world blind."

Friedman, however, puts a different spin on it when he analyzes the historical records of the orthodox Jews. "What is unique in the Hasidic approach to reconciliation is that it points the way to seeing justice and love as necessary complements of each other rather than as alternatives between which one must choose....The large majority of people in our culture hold the distorted view that the God of the Old Testament is a harsh and wrathful God, in contrast to the loving and merciful God of the New.... An 'eye for an eye and a tooth for a tooth' is *not* the expression of a vengeful God but a primitive statement of basic social democracy in which no [one] is held of greater worth than another, because each is created in the image of God....Throughout all history, indeed, the natural *inequality* of man has justified razing a whole city to avenge the murder of one privileged man. Countless others have been exterminated with impunity because they were slaves, or serfs, or members of an 'inferior race.' 'An eye for an eye' is a fundamental conception of social justice" (119).

Where can you see alternatives to revenge articulated? What principles are offered? How would Friedman's analysis help us judge the casualties in conflicts around the world today? In the recent past?

102. Listen to Veterans Talk about Peace

In *Long Shadows: Veterans' Paths to Peace,* Vietnam veteran David Giffey (2006) offers us a collection of autobiographical essays by veterans who are active in the peace movement, although few see themselves as pacifists. Instead, they cry out to stop unnecessary violence perpetrated by politicians and senior commanders far distant from combat but eager for power and honor. From the Spanish Civil War up through the War in Iraq, first-hand experiences in warfare make for heartfelt commitments to an ethic of honest and courageous resistance to what is all too often only the deadly sword rattling bravado of greed exploding into violence.

Robert Kimbrough was a front line marine officer during the Korean War. Listen to his description of what he faced and the conclusions he has had. "For example, and this kind of thing happened more than once, from battalion, we got an assignment that filtered down to one squad of my platoon that had us going deeply behind some strong points of land shooting out toward our lines from the hills where the Chinese were. It was a full moon. There wasn't a cloud in the sky. We had to go out on rice paddies. So I did what most platoon leaders were doing: We went out slowly in a spaced single line. Hunkered down in front of our own lines, I said. 'Okay, everybody be at ease. Be alert.' After an hour or so, I said, 'Okay, fire.' Everybody fired his rifle and trooped back in. I called in a report that we had carried out our mission of assault. 'No casualties. Many enemy killed.' Strictly speaking, I had disobeyed an order. But the order was insane. . . . You've got to watch out for your troops. . . . And those guys would do anything that I would ask them to do, which was very humbling. . . . Again, the senior people plan for their own glory" (46, 47, 49).

How do you connect Kimbrough's experience to your life today? What have you read that offers an inside and deeper perspective on what those in the military have experienced and believed? Describe those situations when you have encountered significant diversity of thought? When differences seemed to be stifled?

103. Take an International Perspective

The path to peace and reconciliation can be blurred by the blinders of local context. Contrasting what we can see around us with what happens overseas can offer striking new insights. In *Long Shadows,* Israeli veteran Esty Dinur (2006) contrasts her experience in the military with what she now sees in the U.S. "I am willing to allow that some people, possibly like (former Israeli military commander and politician Ariel) Sharon . . . really think that militarism is good, that the iron fist is good, and that the Palestinians are really bad. . . . When it comes to the American government, to American presidents, the situation is different. Nobody ever tried to invade the U.S. Directly. . . . To me, having studied history and looked at patterns, to me it's clear that we're talking, more than anything, about economics. We're talking about making money off of other lands. We're talking empire. Even though it looks different from the empires of the nineteenth century, that is what we're looking at" (246).

With the perspective of having lived in Israel before relocating to the U.S., Esty Dinur can see the differences between these two countries quite clearly. In Israel, militarism becomes more understandable because it has been surrounded by hostile nations and factions. But what could explain the extraordinary military preparedness in the U.S., which is protected by oceans to the east and west and has friendly neighbors to the north and the south? Dinur concludes that it must be something else: "economics" and "empire." When you make comparisons between countries on issues of peace and reconciliation, what do you notice? What questions arise for you?

ENCOURAGING CRITICAL THINKING ABOUT ALTERNATIVES TO VIOLENCE

Much is known about critical thinking—how to analyze deductively or build concepts through induction, how to refine those concepts and develop rules and higher-order rules—although assessment is always and inherently more complex, more subjective. There may be multiple paths to a particular solution. As complex and multifaceted concepts, peace and reconciliation represent special challenges. That is all the more reason to take their study seriously and develop a repertoire of instructional skills for addressing each.

Having some abilities to analyze problems, to study the past and apply what is relevant to the future, helps to defuse the emotionality that often surrounds conflicts and allow more reasoned responses to surface. However, we can also make tragic mistakes by applying mistaken analyses and arriving at incorrect conclusions. In the 2004 documentary, *The Fog of War*, Robert McNamara, the Secretary of Defense during much of the Vietnam War, admits to having had the wrong paradigm in mind, i.e., that the U.S. was following the tenets of a "domino theory" orchestrated out of Beijing and Moscow, when what was really going on was a civil war.

Each of the next three activities opens avenues for critical discussion of the relationships that literary characters foster with one another. Those relationships can be related to real world experiences; people can make connections to their own personal relationships or to international politics in a way that can be discerning and engaged. Insight about manifesting peace through dialogue, interpersonal or political action, and study can be sparked by investigating various literary characters.

Teaching literature provides rich opportunities to address issues of power, protracted social conflict, resolution, human rights, and justice. People are particularly engaged when asked to consider relationships between the characters, as well as what motivated the action of the story. The next three "Tips" intend to promote perspective about conflicts in literature and spark conversations about building peace. The first two activities can be used to review a text and capture both imagination and intellect. The third activity can provide entry to critical conversations about peace while a text is being read.

104. Provide a Bird's Eye View of Conflict and Interpersonal Relationships in Literature: Use the Drama Triangle

Karpman's "Drama Triangle" (Diagram 1) can clarify complex relationships where parties play the roles of persecutor, victim, and rescuer. By considering which characters are explicitly or implicitly placing themselves or others at various points on the triangle, people better understand how personal and political interactions can be motivated by and result in fierce complexities. As behaviors are documented on the triangle, viable options for reconciliation present themselves. Language regarding interpersonal and international relationships is honed. By analyzing the ramifications of human words and actions, people can develop their abilities to take a bird's eye view of interactions.

Draw Karpman's triangle on a poster-sized sheet of paper or the board. At one angle write *Victim*, at another, *Persecutor*, and at the final corner, *Rescuer.* Have people move through the character list of, say, *Hamlet,* discussing plot and character traits to figure out which character belongs at which corner: for example, *Is Hamlet a victim? A persecutor? A rescuer? To whom?* People can then usually see the intricate relationships between the characters more clearly, how often the same characters played rescuer for the victim they had persecuted.

Questions for discussion become more intricate. Examples might include:

- How does Hamlet victimize Ophelia?
- Where would Gertrude be placed on the triangle? Is she persecuted or rescued by Claudius, Hamlet, Polonius? Whom does she persecute or rescue?
- Where do we place Rosencrantz and Guildenstern, bearing in mind their intentions and then their demise?

Once the characters have been mapped onto the triangle, it's often clear whether there are gender issues evidenced by which character plays which role. Discussion about the mythologies of gender or power can now begin: the vulnerable maiden, the elder, bitter queen, the benevolent old king, the scheming lord. People might make their own connections to current events, either local or global. Facilitators can then decide, based on context, if they would like to initiate discussions about international or community relations. This model is based on Karpman's Drama Triangle, a tool for Transactional Analysis, which can be found on the website: http://www.karpmandramatriangle.com.

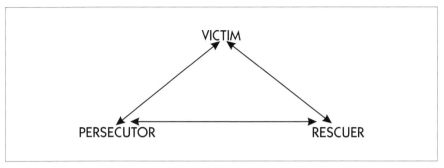

Diagram 1: Drama triangle

105. Use the United Nations' Universal Declaration of Human Rights (UDHR)

The UDHR is a rich enough text to teach peace and justice on its own. When applied to a familiar literary or biographical text, people can gain both familiarity with the application of the UDHR and a deeper understanding of their own text. Compassion for characters can deepen with the hope that compassion for people in their communities will also grow. By placing themselves in the shoes of literary characters, they exercise the ability to see another person's perspective. Hopefully, they will make connections to their communities or to the world-at-large. Again, it is the facilitator's choice, based on context, whether or not to push thinking in that direction.

For example, let's look at Frederick Douglass' autobiography, *My Bondage and My Freedom*. Hand out the United Nations' Universal Declaration of Human Rights. Give everyone a chance to read it and write down examples from the Douglass text that have references in the UDHR. This moment to reflect is important because the discussion can become heated. Writing helps participants remember ideas as the time remaining grows short. The very first article in the UDHR will often raise discussion: "All human beings are born free and equal in rights and dignity."

With respect to Douglass, he was born neither free, nor equal with respect to whites. He was not protected from violations of his dignity. People will often wonder about the extent to which the times and context have changed and bring up contemporary examples. You could ask them to prepare speeches or papers on ways to ensure that human rights are protected. They could discuss individual responsibility and rights in the wake of various political developments or natural disasters. For more, see: http://www.un.org/en/documents/udhr/ index.shtml.

106. Identify Points in Literature where Ego and Status Quo Are Threatened

A third literary analysis activity helps people identify precise moments that generate social conflict, i.e., those moments that might threaten the basic needs of a character and spark a violent reaction. As discussed previously, conflicts can be powerful catalysts for getting to a deeper understanding of peace and reconciliation. For example, in *Hamlet,* some might argue that Hamlet feels initially threatened when the murderer, Uncle Claudius, threatens to take Gertrude's motherly love from the distraught prince. In terms of power issues, some may want to analyze the attachment to control as the genesis of this conflict. By identifying the threats, people can predict subsequent decisions made by main characters that drive the outcome of the drama. Consider alternative routes the characters might have taken to avoid the loss of life. What actions and words could have created an atmosphere of peace and reconciliation?

107. Use an Advance Organizer for Peace and Reconciliation

In *Metateaching and the Instructional Map,* Timpson (1999) draws on the work of David Ausubel to describe the benefits of an overview that can help us see the bigger picture and keep our work toward peace and reconciliation within a meaningful context. Day in and day out, we all face very real challenges in making sense of everything that is coming at us; we have to sort out what we should pay attention to from what we could ignore.

Identifying our own *advance organizers* for resolving conflicts and building understanding can help. "Introducing the idea of the *advance organizer,* David Ausubel (1963) demonstrated the value of a conceptual preview or framework for helping students to organize their thinking and learning. Teachers and texts can help students by laying out the larger underlying concepts, and then make periodic references to those concepts as a foundation for all the facts, figures, and ideas that follow" (26).

Identify those major ideas that guide your thinking about peace and reconciliation and put each in a circle. Draw arrows out to activities that you already do as well as to those you might do. Major ideas represent your advance organizers for peace and reconciliation. Post these where you can see, review, and refine them. For example, knowing that no "weapons of mass destruction" (WMDs) were found after the U.S. invasion of Iraq in 2003 led many to rethink their support and to challenge the explanations that were made in the lead up to the invasion. Re-evaluate your own thinking about that war as well as other wars. Note the value that an analysis of this type on a specific problem has on your thinking.

108. Enhance "Perspective Consciousness" about Diverse Views

In the field of global education, Robert Hanvey (1982) defines his classic term "perspective consciousness" as the "recognition on the part of an individual that he or she has a view of the world that is not universally shared, that this view of the world has been and continues to be shaped by influences that often escape conscious detection, and that others have views of the world that are profoundly different from one's own" (3).

Perspective consciousness emerges as an individual understands the boundaries of "self" and the "other." One's limited views, values, and ways of being in the world are recognized as relative to conscious and unconscious cultural conditionings in one's own situated historical context. The "other's" views, values, and ways of being in the world are recognized as valid and stemming from local conscious and unconscious contextual forces as well. Attaining a culturally relative viewpoint becomes paramount; our students must strive to not judge others based on their own narrow explicit or tacit cultural standards. The recognition, tolerance, understanding, and acceptance of differences between "self" and "other" is extremely important for creating culturally sensitive and culturally responsive citizens and educators (Brantmeier 2003).

Choose a global event or conflict, the more recent the better; e.g., in 2008 we had the Darfur conflict, Iraq conflict, cyclone in Myanmar, earthquake in China, conflict in Tibet. Brainstorm and research multiple interpretations of those conflicts or events by examining various media sources on the Internet. Who are the key players, the key interpreters of the events? What are the vested interests and historical legacies of those key players? How does the media coverage promote a certain "version" of the truth? Whose voice is missing from the coverage? What are the implications of dominant discourses in the media? What message might be sent and interpreted by nations and people in other national and societal contexts? Whose interests does that serve? Create a drawing, chart, or map that illustrates the vested interests of a given global event and/or conflict. Reflect on Hanvey's definition of perspective consciousness above. What insights emerge?

109. Practice Best-Case Thinking about Peace and Reconciliation

In her book, *Cultures of Peace,* Elise Boulding (2000) makes a strong argument for a new paradigm in the way we think, individually and collectively, locally and globally. "In general, societies tend to be a blend of peaceable and warrior culture themes—the balance between the themes varying from society to society and from historical moment to historical moment. In our time, the tensions between the two themes have become a heavy social burden as a worldwide military forcing system linked to a destructive, planet-harming mode of industrialization and urbanization is distorting the human capability for creative and peaceful change. No sooner did the fears of nuclear holocaust fade with the end of the Cold War than the fear of genocidal ethnic warfare reducing once proudly independent countries to a series of dusty battlegrounds rose to take the place of earlier fears. Urban violence—now manifesting itself in gun battles in the cities and neighborhoods and even the schoolyards and playgrounds of the industrial West—has unleashed other terrors. If every society is a blend of the themes of violence and peaceableness, why is the peaceableness so hard to see? It is there, but not well reported. The tendency of planners and policy-makers to prepare for worst-case scenarios leaves societies unprepared for the opportunities involved in best-case scenarios" (4).

Identify a problem you are having. Indulge yourself in some worst-case thinking. Now try some best-case thinking. What insights do you get about each? For many people, worst-case thinking reinforces fear-based responses, a tightening and narrowing of the hard-wired flight-or-fight response. However, when people utilize best-case thinking, they tend to see many more options, an openness to possibility in the present and hope on the horizon. In best-case thinking, there is more openness to explore new and different solutions.

110. Understand Learning Style Preferences for Peacemaking

In *Teaching and Learning Peace,* Timpson (2002) describes the different learning styles that can be useful in understanding why some people are successful and others struggle to master new material, especially when concepts like peace and reconciliation require a degree of sophisticated thought. "Jerome Bruner (1966) has also reported that knowing student preferences for reflection or more impulsive action can be very useful for instructors. For example, you yourself may be the type of person who needs time and space to think through what you hear. When students feel that they need to make an immediate response to an instructor's questions in class, some may feel anxious and/or intimidated. However, learning to speak up and participate actively in discussions can prove enormously valuable, and not just in school. . . . While the peace movement has historically called on a whole range of talents, protests and demonstrations do require a certain willingness to be seen and heard in public" (117-118). Certainly, Gandhi and Thich Nhat Hanh have publicly celebrated the role for meditation in staying centered and clear, especially in times of crises.

For those you know who are more passive and reflective, consider these possibilities:

- People often use the quiet of the library or their own homes to reflect, clarify, organize, and prepare. At a lecture or other presentation, providing them with an explanatory handout can relieve some of the pressure on them to get "every word down."

- It can be useful to provide people some time for them to reflect individually or to meet in small groups to talk over their questions or assignments with one or two others before a general, public discussion begins. In any group, you may have some who seem to learn best by speaking up, who clarify their own thinking through talking. In a large group this can be a problem but one you can satisfy, in part, with regular small group interactions.

- In a group, if a few are dominating the discussions and you want to get others involved, ask for responses from "those who have not participated" or encourage the use of time outside of the meeting or e-mail for more individual issues or concerns.

- Have people make presentations in your meetings about topics of their choosing. Tapping into their interests as well as providing opportunity for them to prepare outside of class will allow those who are quieter to participate more.

- Allow time in class for everyone to reflect and meditate. As happens in Quaker meetings, these periods of quiet can be the source of important personal insights. Silence sometimes speaks volumes.

- Task or study groups can be a wonderful mechanism for active and impulsive people to take proactive responsibility about their own learning styles. Note that the more you can help your students understand their own preferences, the better able they should be to learn with others, to communicate what works for them and what they need to move forward. These skills will then serve them—*and you*—well when you add additional levels of complexity into your meetings.

- You can also help active and impulsive learners develop their reflective abilities by using their notes to write out (and think about) their questions.

111. Use Cooperative, Experiential, and Student-Centered Approaches

Collaborative, field-based and individualized activities can be powerful experiences for learning about peace and reconciliation (Timpson 2002). In the excerpt that follows, note how these varied approaches can help people deepen their understanding of complex and difficult issues. Also note how concern for sustainability can be framed as a desire to make peace with the planet and begin the healing needed.

For a campus course on sustainable design, (Professor Brian) Dunbar took on an actual building project at Colorado State University as the focus for small group collaboration. The resulting activities were varied and complex, impacted by the communication skills of the students as well as by their learning styles, backgrounds and motivations. Opportunities to visit the nearby proposed building site allowed for a student-centered process which seemed to blend the "space" necessary for creativity, both literally and figuratively, with the reality of a particular piece of land. In addition, we realized that we needed time together and a climate of mutual respect to challenge established paradigms and imagine new possibilities. When the Department Head and two of his key faculty members arrived for the presentation on the last day, they saw—and felt—the collective enthusiasm, creativity, and commitment of this group for sustainable design and construction. By allowing the time for this kind of exploration and input, deeply held values about environmentally sustainable practices could be shared and addressed.

Employing similar student-centered practices, Dunbar also recruited a group of students to join him in the U.S. Virgin Islands on St. John to study sustainable design and construction at a resort which itself was internationally famous for following principles of ecological design. Unlike high-end resorts nearby—air conditioners buzzing in solar-oblivious buildings over large and manicured lawns where the local sources of drinking water have all been spoiled—the Maho Bay eco-resort blends tent structures and connecting boardwalks into the existing forested landscape. Students meet and work in open air pavilions that model a much lighter, more respectful relationship to the land. However, while the sunsets were stunning, students were challenged to wrestle with the terrible ecological toll that early European colonizers had exacted, clear cutting the island and expropriating slave labor to make sugar cane production possible and lucrative. Dunbar's use of meditations and music added even more power to the depth of this field-based learning experience. (115)

Identify those times when collaborative, field-based, and individualized experiences helped you get new insights into peace and reconciliation. When have you seen these approaches work with others? Rethink an upcoming event to incorporate aspects of each.

112. Explore the Sounds of Peace

Dean Nelson spent many years in the military and saw much combat. He understands all too well the importance of peace studies. "Peace throughout the world can mean the same, but sound completely different to the ear not accustomed to the language being spoken. Exposing people to the concept of peace and what it means can be a powerful lesson in discovery learning. You can use open-ended questions to assess what people understand about peace and how they came to that understanding."

The peaceCENTER (http://www.salsa.net) offers peace tools for teachers. One of their exercises is called *A New Language of Peace*: "Every language has a word for peace. Greet people with words of peace in many languages and use this as a springboard for discussing the meaning of peace and a world without violence." The exercise involves students greeting other students in a foreign language of their choice, from a list of choices. The class then becomes involved in a deeper discussion of how peace means the same in other languages and what it means to wish other people peace. For example:

English: peace	Farsi: solh	Japanese: heiwa
Afrikaans: vrede	French: paix	Korean: peoning hwa
Catalan: pau	German: der friede	Sioux: wo okeyeh
Hawaiian: malu	Spanish: paz	Danish: fred
Italian: pace	Turkish: baris	Comanche: tsumukikiatu

113. Use Inductive Thinking to Re-Think Problems

Peace and reconciliation often require new ideas and different thinking and, consequently, teaching can truly be transformative. One approach that can help people arrive at new insights is to guide an inductive analysis where data are grouped and re-grouped, old ideas challenged and new concepts created. In *My Pilgrimage to Nonviolence,* Martin Luther King Jr. looked back over the conflicts in the first half of the twentieth century and, instead of seeing collapse and despair, saw something emergent and hopeful. "We who live in the twentieth century are privileged to live in one of the most momentous periods of human history. It is an exciting age, filled with hope. It is an age in which a new social order is being born. We stand today between two worlds—the dying old and the emerging new. Now I am aware of the fact that there are those who would contend that we live in the most ghastly period of human history. They would argue that the rhythmic beat of the deep rumblings of discontent from Asia, the uprisings in Africa, the nationalistic longings of Egypt, the roaring cannons from Hungary, and the racial tensions of America are all indicative of the deep and tragic midnight which encompasses our civilization. They would argue that we are retrogressing instead of progressing. But far from representing retrogression and tragic meaninglessness, the present tensions represent the necessary pains that accompany the birth of anything new" (King 2000, 178).

This inductive process for King began with a listing of the violence he was seeing both near and far. However, instead of accepting the despairing interpretations that he was hearing from others, he chose to organize this "data" differently and see something much more hopeful. Yes, there was a coming apart, but for King these events also meant a "birth" of freedom, a coming out for those seeking independence from the older colonial powers. Without trivializing the violence that accompanied these changes, King recognized these "pains" as necessary for the emergence of the new order.

In *Concepts and Choices for Teaching,* Timpson and Doe (2008) describe the inductive process. Try a similar process for yourself or with others. Begin with a listing of conflicts that you can see—global, national, regional or local, personal or interpersonal. What would most people conclude? Now group these conflicts in ways that lead to a different conclusion. Move issues around until new groupings emerge. Try various labels. Step back and look for possible relationships. Hypothesize what may be the underlying concepts. For example, consider the "get tough" policies that have filled U.S. prisons at the turn of the twenty-first century. An analysis of offenses would show that many inmates are in prison because of drug offenses and addiction. Two fundamental questions emerge: What are the consequences, both positive and negative, if we de-criminalize addiction and use a therapeutic approach instead? How would cost be affected?

114. Explore Critical and Controversial Issues

Few people really enjoy conflict. That's one argument for peace. Yet, re-treat from tough issues rarely solves a problem. Instead, there is everything to gain from knowing how to face problems, handle the attendant emotions and explore possible solutions. A long-time advocate of a culture of care, Nel Noddings (2003) encourages us to develop these abilities. "If we value critical thinking, if we commit ourselves to encouraging it, then we must allow it to be exercised on critical matters. . . . If we really believe that knowledge and critical thinking contribute to living fuller public and private lives, then we must allow the study and discussion of such critical and controversial issues" (148).

Discovery learning is a well studied approach that provides a framework for exploration, helping people identify a problem, consider various approaches, test their ideas, and decide on a way forward. Yet, success with discovery also requires that we learn how to manage our emotions, channel our anxieties, and deal with the challenges we face. When have you faced a conflict or controversy and discovered useful insights? How can we help others to do the same?

115. Get Past Your Biases and Open Up to New Insights

As an African American who grew up in the deep south, Will Williams (2006) seethed with anger and hatred for what he had seen done to black people. He grew up in the army in Vietnam, recognizing his own racism. "When I first got there, I didn't see them as Vietnamese. I'd been brainwashed. I saw them as the enemy. I had no regard for their life. I used to call them 'books,' the word that I hate to hear now. It bothers me when people use it. But back then, I was doing it. It took a lot of years for me to realize that I was doing to them the same thing that had been done to me in Mississippi verbally. That word 'good' is the same as being called 'nagger' in Mississippi, and I was guilty of it. So it just re-inforced the fact that I was brainwashed, that I was used as other veterans are used. I hadn't realized that the system had beaten my brain to that point where I didn't see people as people until many years later" (82).

As a professor of comparative religions, Jim Boyd (2003) has had to explore various ways to help students unlearn their prejudices, including getting past his own ego. Like Williams, he had to do some intense soul-searching. "I have found over the years that the less ego I bring into the classroom, the more my students and I connect with the ideas being discussed. In those successful moments when I manage to weave the conceptual and emotional fabric of another worldview, there is an interesting sense in which 'I' am not present" (72).

What "brainwashing" have you had to untangle? When has "ego" gotten in the way of your efforts to see new insights or address problems in different ways?

116. Construct, Deconstruct, and Reconstruct Attitudes

In *Teaching Diversity*, Val Middletown (2003) describes her work in challenging her students and herself to address issues of prejudice, discrimination, inequity, injustice, and all those "isms" that compromise learning, undermine basic democratic principles, and perpetuate conflicts. Note how her conclusions about diversity could so easily be applied to work for peace and reconciliation. "Diversity courses in teacher education present a unique set of issues for instructors. . . .I often have to evaluate my own preparation and ability. . . .I must be able to process both the students' issues and my own. . . .Anger, fear, silence, vehemence, avoidance, guilt, passion, enthusiasm, and many other constructive and unconstructive emotions and reactions can erupt as we construct, deconstruct, and reconstruct our attitudes and beliefs about diversity" (103).

Examine your own ideas and feelings about peace and reconciliation today. What has changed over time? Which have you "constructed" from your own unique experiences? Which have you had to "deconstruct" because old attitudes had proven problematic? Which have you had to "reconstruct" because of what you inherited from others?

117. Hear and Respect Other Voices

In *Long Shadows,* Vietnam veteran Joel Garb (2006) describes how he changed while serving in the military during wartime, how he benefitted from seeking different opinions. "I decided to join the Army even though by that time I was relatively certain that the war was wrong. And yet there was so much official propaganda that I felt like I should go see for myself. Not having much common sense, I didn't realize that you can't see a lot from the perspective of a soldier in a war. You can't see a lot about the causes and reasons for a war when you're in a war. And yet I was fortunate enough to actually meet a Vietnamese man, a colonel, who had been involved in Vietnam's politics since he completed high school and joined the Viet Minh in 1944 or 1945. And so I learned a lot about Vietnam, and the things that he told me reinforced what I already thought, that it was wrong to be there and that we were acting criminally, that our country was acting criminally, and that our soldiers were acting criminally" (182).

Early on, Garb realized that he needed to look beyond what he was being told by official Army sources and learn for himself. For example, he was always deeply troubled by the common reference to the Vietnamese people as "books." He now appreciates the perspectives of his new allies that much more. "And I think that's one thing that distinguishes people that are in Veterans for Peace is that we do have a sense that we're the same as others. We do not appreciate, what's the word, this dehumanization of the so-called enemy or the people that are different from us" (184).

Evaluate your own perspectives about the wars and "enemies" you have heard about in your lifetime. What has changed? Why? What prejudices have you held against people who are different? Who are your role models for seeing people without prejudice?

118. Confront the Violence in Language

In his often provocative book on writing, *Walking on Water,* Derrick Jensen (2004) challenges the reader to confront greed and make peace with the planet. In one exercise, he asks students to come up with the writing prompts and questions. "One group included a Vietnam vet. On their night he and one other student wrote on one chalkboard the words *patriotism, heroism, war, bomb, national defense, national interest, missiles, tanks, guns, helicopters, soldiers, generals.* Simultaneously two other group members wrote on another chalkboard, right next to the first, the words *funk, prick, cut, sex, come, tit.* We went around the room giving our reactions to the words on the two lists. The point soon became clear: why, they were asking, are the words on the second list considered obscene, while the first are not?" (146)

When Bill Timpson tried this exercise with a graduate class, the discussion went even further. One young father noted how the concepts on the "military" side protected the "freedoms" that made the "free speech" of the "sex" list possible. Another wondered about a culture that was "so uptight about sex"? Another noted an "emotionality" with the "sex" list that was absent in the other. One experienced teacher saw the "sex" list as "life producing" while the "military" list was ultimately "life destroying."

Reflect on your own reactions to these lists. Add other words and note your reactions. Use a "free write" and let your writing help you explore your own thinking and emotions. Experiment with other kinds of lists.

119. Explore Shakespeare

There is much in Shakespeare that has proven timeless and much, in particular, that speaks of war and peace, loyalty, betrayal, and reconciliation. *Julius Caesar,* for example, raises questions about empire and power, control, and the influence of the wealthy oligarches versus that of the merchants and farmers. Built on the exploitation of slaves and conquered peoples, the Roman Empire can also be studied for its contributions to architecture and road building, language, and cultural vigor. In Caesar's time, there was heightened competition for the allegiance of the soldiers and the people as competing forces in Rome were pitted against the power of the armies in far off lands. Once Caesar was assassinated, however, Rome tilted more toward the concentration of power in the next emperor, Caesar Augustus.

There are many examples we can look to around the planet but the comparisons between the Republican and Democratic parties in the run up to the U.S. presidential elections in 2008 seemed to reflect a similar divide between an ever more powerful executive under George W. Bush and his war on terror versus the more popular appeal of an Obama candidacy, his opposition to the War in Iraq, and his stated desire to roll back the tax breaks of the wealthiest five percent. Despite the record of deficits and government built up during Republican administrations—Reagan, Bush father and son—John McCain continued to bang on the traditional critique of the Democrats as the party of "tax and spend." Bill Clinton's record of government surpluses and eight years of peace stand in stark contrast to what occurred during the presidency of George W. Bush.

What other lessons about war and peace, violence, and reconciliation can you see in *Julius Caesar?* In the other works of Shakespeare?

120. Make Peace with the Planet

In his Honors seminar on peacemaking, Bill Timpson wanted his students to stretch and connect their studies of conflict management, communication across differences, critical and creative thinking, and teamwork to a range of compelling issues. His students had already read about David Orr's (1994) insistence in *Earth in Mind* that the U.S. preoccupation with growth and consumption had become a major threat to the environment. Orr had written: "The truth is that many things on which our future health and prosperity depend are in dire jeopardy" (7).

For Timpson, then, asking students to write on "making peace with the planet" was a topic that they had already considered and their responses were thoughtful, personally meaningful, and a few were even stunning. One student wrote: "It is wonderful that our country is trying to be more environmentally friendly with canvas shopping bags and hybrid cars, and that we're attempting to make peace with the planet. I just hope that our efforts will be enough, but I can't help but wonder if everyone is up to the challenge. I don't know if enough people would be willing to try and reduce our consumption. All I think I can do is start with myself and hope that others will follow my example. I can reduce the impact I'm having right now." And then she asked: "What will you do to make peace with the planet? Are you up to the challenge?"

In class, after Timpson returned their papers, there was some discussion about possible actions. "Everyone acknowledged that each person could model a more peaceful relationship with the planet. However, we also talked about the systemic changes that would be needed on a host of levels—economic, political, cultural—for the focus on consumption to shift."

How would you make peace with the planet?

121. Question Reality and Accept Responsibility

In *Walking on Water,* Derrick Jensen (2004) notes the "surface" humanity that could be found even in the bowels of the Nazi death machine. "Robert Jay Lipton, probably the world's foremost authority on the psychology of genocide, made clear in his crucial book *The Nazi Doctors* that many of the physicians working at concentration camps such as Auschwitz attempted to make life as comfortable as they could for their charges, doing everything in their power to save inmates' lives, except the most important thing of all: questioning the Auschwitz reality, that is, the atrocity-inducing superstructure under which they operated (often without anesthetic)."

Jensen then fast forwards to his own role—and the responsibility of everyone—in helping to support a materialistic culture in the U.S. that is far too wasteful of natural resources and puts far too many toxins into our air, water, and soil in the name of development and profit. "The fact that industrial education murders souls instead of bodies doesn't reduce my culpability. . . . As much as I may wish to pretend I'm helping to take down civilization, when I teach at a university I'm actually training the future technocrats who will prop up civilization and who, by simply doing their jobs as well and perhaps as good-heartedly as I do mine, will commit genocide the world over and eviscerate what still remains of the natural world" (191).

Identify those "deeper" structures—the political, economic, social, cultural, and environmental—that could be questioned. Identify areas where you can accept responsibility for "propping up" what, in truth, needs to change.

PROMOTING CREATIVITY

People can become frozen in their thinking about peace and reconciliation, locked into the ways that they have been taught to think or brought up to believe. Thomas Kuhn (1970) framed some of these moments as reflective of "paradigm shifts," when one way of thinking gives way to another. For example, in the documentary *The Fog of War*, former Secretary of Defense Robert McNamara admits that the U.S. had the wrong idea in mind when it went to war in Vietnam, that there was no communist master plan orchestrated by Moscow or Beijing whereby the various nations of Southeast Asia would fall like "dominos." Rather, this was a civil war. It is because the costs of war and violence are so high that creativity is especially important at every level of society, from the individual to the organization, from the community to the state, the nation, and every organization of nations.

122. Use Stories to Engage and Teach

In *Teaching and Learning Peace,* Bill Timpson (2002) describes the various ways in which skilled storytelling help to make the history surrounding work toward peace and reconciliation more real, more alive and engaging. "Stories can be powerfully simple mechanisms to engage audiences and stimulate learning. The rich details of lives, events, and places draw us in and speak volumes about underlying beliefs and values. Without analysis or judgment, we are left to come to our own conclusions, much like audiences in the theater. Given the controversies that often surround peace activists, stories can be a powerful ally, for example, as they confront a government's war-making propaganda machinery and attempt to challenge mindless or misplaced patriotism" (107).

Timpson goes on to describe the opportunities any of us has for developing our abilities as story-tellers. "Entire associations have grown up to keep the ancient traditions of storytelling alive. Books have been written and workshops offered to those who want to develop these skills. With practice, teachers at all levels can learn to use their voices more effectively, to add inflection, to adjust their timing and add pauses for reflection. The simplest gesture can add emphasis. A simple prop or bit of clothing can enhance an effect. Attention to this level of detail can augment any message, making the embedded "lessons" so much more memorable. [See *Teaching and Performing,* Timpson and Bourgogne 2002, for more on storytelling.] Like other forms of performance, telling stories brings a personal and human side to lessons and discussions, especially important when we are attempting to de-program those otherwise addicted to violence as a preferred response to conflict" (109).

Assess your own abilities as a storyteller. Organize a session for people to share stories about peace and reconciliation, conflict, and violence. Offer each other feedback about the effectiveness of these stories and what could be improved. Offer ideas about simple gestures or facial expressions, about vocal changes or pauses. Rehearse each story for a more polished presentation. Use audio- or videotaping. What questions or prompts work best for generating deeper audience responses?

123. Use "Sculpting Reality" and "Utopia" to Generate New Insights

If too many are frozen in old ways of thinking about peace and reconciliation, tapping other modalities could light new "fires" and spark new insights. Building on the work of fellow Brazilian Paulo Freire (1970) and his groundbreaking book on literacy education, *Pedagogy of the Oppressed,* Boal (1979, 1992, 1995) began exploring ways in which the theater could be used to raise issues and experiment with new and different responses.

One technique he developed in the context of the "theater of the oppressed" is to use *sculpting* to see an issue from a physical, nonverbal, and, hopefully, new perspective. People are recruited from the audience to play various still-life roles in a scene that captures the essence of a particular problem. For example, someone wants to stage a protest of an extremely violent film at a local movie theater. Some volunteers are placed outside the theater box office protesting—perhaps holding signs, or challenging theater goers to avoid a particular film, or yelling something. Others might be positioned in line to buy tickets but reacting to the protest—annoyed or angry at being bothered; confused or sympathetic. Once in place and in character, everyone, including observers, has a few moments to absorb the impact of this "still life." In a second sculpture, the protest has had some effect and patrons of the theater have turned away from this film or joined the protest. Again, allow a few moments for everyone to absorb the implications of this scene. Then the questions for the debriefing: What insights came from the two scenes? What does it take for people to shift from mindless consumption of violence to actual rejection? What is the best form of protest?

Have someone volunteer a current problem or conflict that he or she would like some help with. Have that person "sculpt" what this problem looks like at its worst by positioning others in a still-life scene. Now have that person transform the scene into what it would like if it were resolved. Return to the original "sculpture" of the problem at its worst and, with the clap of your hands, have each person in the scene make a move toward the ideal. During the debriefing, ask for insights from the original volunteer: What was noticed or felt? What new insights emerged?

For Ellyn Dickmann, having students play with notions of "Reality" and "Utopia" can also open up new insights. She writes: "In a classroom setting, it is often difficult to create the 'perfect' world solution because, as students remind me, 'Reality gets in the way!' I have found that when working with case studies or problems, the inclusion of 'Utopia' group thinking produces better outcomes. In a graduate policy development and analysis class, I had students develop implementation plans for recently introduced state level policy. I created two groups—'Reality' and 'Utopia.' Groups self-selected and worked in separate rooms and were asked to create a plan to implement a proposed state level policy regarding the types of food that could be served for public school lunches. The 'Reality' group worked with all of the traditional boundaries that they perceived to exist such as limited money, staffing, and other resources. In contrast, the 'Utopia' group was asked to create an implementation plan that had no boundaries. The 'Reality' group reported out to the entire class first and then the 'Utopia' group presented and discussion followed. Both groups were surprised by the creative and valuable thinking that was generated by the 'Utopia' group and how exciting and workable the final shared plan was."

On the next occasion that you address a problem, play with this notion of "Reality" and "Utopia" and see what emerges. Critical and creative thinking can develop with these kinds of "stretching" activities.

124. Create "Spect-Actors" to Explore New Insights

Augusto Boal (1979, 1992, 1995) described various ways in which actors could use the experiences that audience members had with conflicts and problems to generate material for the "performance" on that day and offer new ideas about peace and reconciliation. Spectators would become "spect-actors." Every "show" would be fresh, real, and relevant. There would be no written scripts, just what the actors are able to coax from those attending. The struggles, challenges, hopes, and dreams of audience members themselves become the focus for improvisations. Scenes are "acted out" by actors—used primarily to jump start a scene—and recruits from the audience. Whoever volunteered the issue gets to see other perspectives and possibilities.

Using the ideas and techniques of Augusto Boal, a lesson on peace education and nonviolence might look like the following: First, students (or any audience member for that matter) are invited to suggest problems for the group. According to Boal, these should be real and complex. With everyone's input, new and different solutions will be explored in a variety of ways. For example, someone might want to work on a conflicted relationship that threatens to turn violent. A parent might want to help a child confront a bully at school. Someone else is frustrated with the sensationalized media coverage of crime.

Then, the one with the "issue" or "problem" chooses individuals to play particular roles. The parent in the example above might pick someone to be the student and someone else to be the bully. The "scene" would be set and the action begun. Note that having participation from people with some acting experience can be helpful to get things going. At any point, however, anyone from the audience can yell "STOP" and jump into any of the roles. After each run through you want to ask the person with the problem: "What was new? Was it believable? What did you learn?" Again, the goal is to give the person with the issue multiple and different perspectives along with some new ideas for resolution. The action is usually fast so you have to make sense of it all on the fly. Everyone gets involved. It's relevant and the audience is both cast and crew.

125. Use Performance to Engage Audiences

Jesuit priest Daniel Berrigan frequently made headlines with his brother Phillip and others by staging protests during the Vietnam War. Convinced that the war was immoral, the Berrigans staged a variety of dramatic events that they hoped would get the attention of both the media and the public. Given the power and resources of governments to control the news and what the Berrigans perceived to be a public too far removed from the horrors of that war, it is easy to see why they chose strategies with high dramatic appeal. "Raising the stakes" is a concept that playwrights use when creating characters and situations that they hope will engage audiences: who or what is at risk and will the audience care?

Here Dan Berrigan (2000) describes their tactics at the Pentagon: "Our purpose there was to bring home to the authorities the meaning and consequences of their decisions to build and sell weapons around the world, thus depriving the poor of life and the right use of the world. We used, as is usual in our efforts, a range of ways of communicating. Some distribute leaflets and carry on conversations with Pentagon employees. Some wear costumes and play the parts of specters of death, walking through the Pentagon concourses, the acres of shops and restaurants and banks beneath the military offices, chanting 'death, death, death, the bomb, the bomb, the bomb.' Still others poured blood, our own blood, which earlier had been gathered clinically by a nurse in the group. The blood was poured out on pillars, walls, doorways, the floor—a terrific amount of blood dripping everywhere. And ashes were poured as well: a sign of our readiness to burn the living. A number of people fell as if dead into the blood and ashes. We carried a cross on which the names of various weapons had been written: trident, cruise missile, neutron bomb, nuclear warhead, napalm. . .all the machinery of death" (95).

List the demonstrations and protests that have gotten your attention in the past. Assess their effectiveness. What role(s) did you play? Could you play? What would limit your involvement? What performance ideas could energize work for peace and reconciliation today?

126. Take the Bus

Living in the Rocky Mountain West, Bill Timpson has had relatively easy access to several national parks. Just an hour and a half from his home in Fort Collins is Rocky Mountain National Park, one of the crown jewels of the system, visited by thousands every year who come from all over the world. You can literally feel the peacefulness as people slow down to drink in these stunning vistas, the mountains and snowy summits, the streams and beaver dams, the hawks, marmots, and picas. The only drawback is the car culture that often creates rush-hour-like traffic.

What a welcome change when Timpson got to visit Zion National Park in Southeastern Utah, where visitors had been overwhelming the space available. Back in the 1950s, this park had thousands of visitors daily competing for the 300-400 car spaces that were available. Faced with the impossibility of this degree of access to private vehicles, the Park Service put in place a shuttle system that has everyone park down below. These buses run every ten minutes from early until late and the calm is palpable. As important, there is this sense of community as you see some of the same people at different stops. You check in about this trail or that. At Rocky Mountain National park, that degree of community just does not happen.

On your next trip, make peace with the planet and use public transportation as much as possible. Note the greater sense of community and your own reactions. Experiment with driving your car less and car pooling more. Notice how you tend to wave to others when you are on your bicycle. At their core, peace and reconciliation involve community. Be more conscious of how being in your car can isolate you. Perhaps, it may lead you to "take the bus" and be more participatory in this world. You can also ask people to identify places in their communities and regions where more use could be made of public transportation. Ask them to work in groups to draft a plan of action, perhaps beginning with a letter campaign to civic leaders.

127. Drumming for Peace: Health and Music Therapy

Music has been used effectively as an alternative therapy or a complementary therapy for patients suffering from addictions. Specifically, drumming has been used for patients who have repeatedly relapsed and have failed with other therapies. In a recent study, Winkelman (2003) examined drumming activities as part of addiction treatment. His research indicated that drumming can speed recovery through relaxation and increased theta-wave production and brainwave synchronization. Drumming can also be great fun, allowing for real release from past emotional trauma. Drumming in a group can help overcome feelings of isolation and alienation, creating a sense of connection with others. Finally, Winkelman reported that drumming could help some connect to a spiritual power.

Katy Kirk studied music therapy at Colorado State University and used it in her work with the Larimer County Center for Mental Health. She found the drumming groups to be highly effective for gaining rapport, as well as for providing an alternative to traditional "talk therapy." As all of this research shows, music can be really important for our health. Music can keep us at peace with ourselves as we improve our mental, physical, emotional, and spiritual states. Beyond this, we can use music as a part of the peacemaking process with others.

Attend a drum circle or learn how to facilitate drum circles in your community. Discuss how the many voices of the drum can contribute to the whole.

USING A DEVELOPMENTAL & VALUES PERSPECTIVE

Developmentalists like Erikson, Piaget, Bruner, Perry, Kohlberg, and Gilligan offer us useful frameworks for understanding the stages and sequences that humans travel as they grow and mature in their thinking. Knowing about this becomes especially important when "fight or flight" is so deeply wired in our psyches, when so much about war and so little about peace constitute our study of history.

128. Take a Developmental Approach

Recognize that people develop in their thinking. Everyone moves from concrete learning through touch and taste as an infant to an increasing use of vision, language, and logic. With maturation they can also increase their ability to go beyond dichotomous judgments (right/wrong, black/white) and see the real world in all its colors of complexity and ambiguity. They can develop their capacity to understand other perspectives, clarify what they believe, and even rethink their own positions given new information or ideas.

Design an activity that requires hands-on, active, and interactive learning. For example, you could pick a date in history that calls for celebration of peace and reconciliation—e.g., the end of a war, the birth of a peacemaker, the signing of a peace treaty, the start of a "Truth and Reconciliation Inquiry." Create a survey about the meaning of that date, that person, etc., for people in your school, on your campus, or in your community. Have students distribute, collect, and analyze the results. You could also have them conduct structured interviews or focus groups. Compile a final report that summarizes everything collected.

129. Examine Values

Values underlie thinking and action yet are often considered off limits for direct instruction in the public classroom. The U.S. tradition that insists on a separation of church and state leaves most educators unsure about their role in addressing values. Anyone teaching can attempt to identify what underlies specific actions, but such an attempt can become speculative and a potential source of controversy. For example, the U.S. invasion of Iraq in 2003 could be seen as a reflection of an aggressive value of the Bush administration—using a pretext like the September 11th attacks to justify sending in the military and extending American control over the Middle East and its rich oil reserves. Alternatively, the Iraq invasion could also be seen as reflecting a value claimed within the Bush administration for defending America's national interests.

Note the focus on values in Martin Luther King's words below. "[In] all his speeches, King's voice was heard calling for what he described as 'a revolution in values' in the United States, a struggle to free ourselves from the 'triple evils of racism, extreme materialism, and militarism.' . . .By the end of the fall (of 1967), King's voice...was setting forth a jarring theme, declaring, 'Something is wrong with capitalism as it now stands in the United States. We are not interested in being integrated into *this* value structure. Power must be relocated....We've got to make it known that until our problem is solved, America may have many, many days, but they will be full of trouble. There will be no rest; there will be no tranquility in this country, until the nation comes to terms with our problems'" (Harding 2000, 198-199).

Introducing a values framework can provide a useful mechanism for analyzing and discussing the range of values that might underline an issue and those involved. For example, at the lowest levels, we can choose our values freely and form alternatives after considering the consequences. At levels three and four, we can prize our values and affirm them publicly. At the highest levels, we act on our values, repeatedly and consistently. Facilitating this kind of analysis can allow individuals to come to their own conclusions and avoid any hint of proselytizing by instructors.

At the end of the day, however, we must also recognize the fundamental importance of tenure and academic freedom in our schools, colleges, and universities, so that our democracy can have the free and open discussions, at least in these venues, it requires to remain healthy. The 2008 September-October issue of *Academe,* the Bulletin of the American Association of University Professors (AAUP), has an excellent range of articles on tenure in higher education, although the principles are relevant at every level of education and in every context of organizational and democratic vitality.

130. Identify Contradictions

Wars are often cloaked in ideals but sparked by the realities of power, greed, and exploitation. Pointing out differences between ideals and realities seems honest and correct yet, in practice, the results will often make people uncomfortable or upset. Assertiveness skills may be needed to raise the issues in the face of entrenched and powerful opponents. Since local public schools, in particular, are "thin skinned" as sociologists like to say and, thereby, subject to pressures from various constituent groups, some diplomacy skills may be needed, i.e., mediation and negotiation skills. Addressing contradictions with integrity and sensitivity will require basic communication skills from everyone, i.e., deep listening, empathy, acceptance, and understanding.

In *A Different Mirror,* Ron Takaki (1993) notes how public education raised the hopes and aspirations of recent immigrant children who saw the contradictions between the ideals of citizenship that were celebrated in American history with the realities of life on the sugar plantations in Hawaii. "Many schools...were not preparing these children to be plantation laborers. They were learning about freedom and equality and reciting the Gettysburg Address and the Declaration of Independence. 'Here the children learn about democracy, or at least the theory of it,' said a University of Hawaii student. They were taught that honest labor, fair play, and industriousness were virtues. But they 'saw that it wasn't so on the plantation.' They saw whites on the top and Asians on the bottom. Returning from school to their camps, students noticed the wide 'disparity between theory and practice.' This contradiction was glaring. 'The public school system, perhaps without realizing it,' the university student observed, 'created unrest and disorganization'" (265).

When have lessons about the ideals of democracy and the realities of inequity created "unrest and disorganization" for you? How do we best teach these contradictions? One way is to focus on case study analysis and model the full and open discussions that underlie critical and creative thinking. As another example, consider the claim in the U.S. that schools are a powerful mechanism for upward mobility. Although this has certainly been true for some, perhaps many, the reality is that school funding policy in the U.S. is tied primarily to the local tax base and, consequently, per pupil expenditures are wildly unequal when wealthy suburbs are contrasted with poor rural and inner city communities. Extend this comparison to other developed nations where funding for schools is equitable and set at a national level, and we can see this glaring contradiction between an expressed ideal in the U.S. and the reality as practiced. The claim of "meritocracy," that less talented and motivated students in the U.S. fail to thrive in a competitive environment and, therefore, end up in poor communities, seems shallow when the disparities in per pupil expenditure are so great. We can also add to this case study the fact that, on average, students in many developed nations have consistently outperformed U.S. students on various standardized exams, especially in math and science. (For a concise summary of these issues with related links and sources, see: www.wikipedia.org/wiki/Education_in_the_United_States.)

131. Insist on Integrity

While violence can arise out of corruption, a sustainable peace typically demands integrity of the highest order. Rampant cheating at U.S. colleges and universities, however, can undermine the moral underpinnings of their role and mission with dangerous consequences for teaching about violence, peace, or reconciliation. In *Teaching Tips,* their classic text on college-level instruction, McKeachie and Svinicki (2006) note that pervasive cheating only engenders greater cynicism among students. "The research on this question is alarmingly consistent. The most significant factor in a student's decision to cheat is peer influence. . . . [Scholars] report that students don't believe they'll get caught because instructors are indifferent to their activities. [Another] reports students' belief that if they do get caught they won't be punished severely, even if the institution has policies for dealing with such misconduct. In today's high-stakes testing environment, where there is such a strong emphasis on grades, students believe there is a large reward for success at any cost. . . . Certainly they see on the news successful cheaters in the real world constantly getting away without severe penalties" (115).

Given the above, assess the integrity of your own organizations and the various groups you support. Is integrity an issue at any level or are there violations that are routinely overlooked? Is peer pressure a factor? Is it only about getting caught or the fear of being prosecuted? Does the modeling "in the real world" affect motivations? And finally, how does all this impact the ability of your students and the people in your organizations or groups to think about peace and reconciliation?

UNDERSTANDING & BUILDING CURRICULUM

Much is known about curricula that engage, inspire, and transfer. The Quakers and Mennonites have been practicing pacifism for generations. During every war in the U.S., groups re-emerge to teach about the conscientious objector status. On the other side, the various military forces continue to research and develop their own training so that troops can adapt to challenges in the field. Curriculum is in our schools, colleges, and universities; it is also in our faith and nonprofit organizations, governmental agencies, businesses, and industries. With that said, there is need for a transformative curriculum to build peace and reconciliation in every organization.

132. Understand Curriculum Development

Elise Boulding (2000) reminds us of how unbalanced the teaching of history typically is, how our curricula too often define eras by the wars that were waged, and how little attention is paid to the curricula of peace, reconciliation, and nonviolent conflict resolution. Kenneth Henson (2006) overviews the history of curriculum development and then lays out the basics from identification of *aims, goals, and objectives* to the creation of a meaningful *activity,* to the *evaluation* of both *products* (projects, exam results, papers, etc.) and *processes* (communication, teamwork, creativity). When addressing various issues and conflicts that have plagued the U.S., Henson notes the central role that educators and curriculum can play: "Historically, teachers have been poorly prepared to address the increasingly diverse nature of our society. Textbooks not only have failed to address this issue, but they have actually contributed to the problem by promoting unacceptable stereotypes and prejudices" (363).

Examine an article, school or college text for controversies, problems, conflicts, and/or tensions that are neglected or poorly addressed. Outline a "lesson" that would raise awareness about this issue. Follow the following guidelines:

- Set a clear *goal,* a general *aim,* and a learning *objective*, i.e., "those involved will be able to…"

- Identify an *activity* that might be relevant and meaningful.
- Determine how this could be *evaluated* for both *product* (knowledge and skills) and *process* (thinking, creating, and cooperating).
- If possible, trial your "lesson," solicit feedback, and refine your ideas further.

133. Deepen Learning within the Cognitive Domain

Understanding how our values and actions build from beliefs and knowledge can help deepen learning about peace and reconciliation. In *Curriculum Planning*, Henson (2006) describes how instructors can make use of what Benjamin Bloom and his colleagues (1956) described as an *educational taxonomy*, putting learning within a hierarchy of difficulty or challenge.

- At level 1 is *knowledge,* the "mastery of facts and concepts" as a "prerequisite for performing higher mental operations."
- At level 2 is *comprehension,* "requiring students to do more than memorize, . . . to translate, interpret, or predict a continuation of trends."
- At level 3 is *application,* requiring students to "use principles or generalizations to solve a concrete problem."
- At level 4 is *analysis,* requiring students to "work with principles, concepts, and broad generalizations."
- At level 5 is *synthesis,* requiring students to "take principles apart, ...to take several parts of something and put them together to make a whole."
- And at level 6 is *evaluation,* requiring students to "make judgments based on definite criteria, not just opinions" (Hansen 2006, 186-189).

Apply these levels from the cognitive domain to the study of a passage from an important peacemaker. For example, examine Martin Luther King, Jr.'s writings on the *interdependence* that holds us all together, that we can recognize and appreciate if we understand more about our daily tasks. "All (people) are interdependent. Every nation is an heir of a vast treasury of ideas and labor to which both the living and the dead of all nations have contributed. Whether we realize it or not, each of us lives eternally 'in the red.' We are everlasting debtors to known and unknown men and women. When we arise in the morning, we go into the bathroom where we reach for the sponge which is provided for us by a Pacific Islander. We reach for soap which is created for us by a European. Then at the table we drink coffee which is provided for us by a South American, or tea by a Chinese, or cocoa by a West African. Before we leave for our jobs we are already beholden to more than half the world" (King 1984, 18).

What knowledge is important in this passage? What understanding? How does King apply the concept of interdependence? What does his analysis reveal? What other sources does he draw upon? How does he evaluate the importance of *interdependence*?

134. Understand Engagement, Values, and the Affective Domain

Violence arouses strong reactions and feelings—aggression, anger, revenge, sorrow, remorse. In our schools and colleges, in particular, there are emotional and value components to learning that are often overlooked when we focus too much on tested outcomes. We need to care about a topic at the very outset or learning becomes drudgery, a routine, something to survive. Kenneth Henson (2006) draws on the work of Krathwohl et al. (1964) to describe the *affective domain* that underlies learning.

- Level 1 is *receiving,* which describes someone's "awareness of new information or experiences."

- Level 2 is *responding,* where a student "reacts to whatever has attracted his or her attention."

- Level 3 is *valuing,* which is "demonstrated when someone prizes a behavior enough to be willing to perform it even in the face of alternatives."

- Level 4 is *organizing,* requiring "individuals to bring together different values to build a value system."

- Level 5 is *characterizing,* where people also "demonstrate a degree of individuality and self-reliance" (Hansen, 2006, 196-197).

We can apply these levels from the affective domain to some written work on peace and reconciliation. For example, read through some of Martin Luther King, Jr.'s writings on *alienation*, those feelings that arise when we believe that our basic values are under assault or unreflective of current political, social, and cultural norms. "When an individual is no longer a true participant, . . . (when) culture is degraded, . . . when the social system does not build security but induces peril, inexorably the individual is impelled to pull away from a soulless society. This process produces alienation—perhaps the most pervasive and insidious development in contemporary society" (King 1984, 19).

How do you *receive* this passage? Are you aware of alienation? How do you *respond*? What is your reaction? How does King show his *value* for peace and reconciliation by analyzing alienation? How does he draw on various values to build his case against alienation? How does he *characterize* his understanding of alienation? How does he demonstrate his own individuality?

135. Be Mindful about Action

From role plays to simulations to meditations, there are many activities and exercises that can deepen and extend learning about peace and reconciliation. In *Curriculum Planning,* Kenneth Henson (2006) draws on the work of Simpson (1972) to describe a useful hierarchy for the potential role of activity.

- At level 1 is *perception* where "phenomena act as guides to motor activity. The individual must first become aware of a stimulus, pick up on cues for action, and then act upon these cues."
- At level 2, *set* refers to an "individual's readiness to act."
- At level 3, a *guided response* may be needed in the beginning when students must use complex skills.
- At level 4, *mechanism* means that we can perform an act "somewhat automatically without having to pause to think through each separate step."
- At level 5, *complex overt responses* involve "more complicated tasks."
- At level 6, *adaptation* requires individuals to "adjust performance as different situations dictate."
- And at level 7, *organization* means that someone can "create new movement patterns to fit the particular situation" (Henson 2006, 198-199).

As instructors or group leaders, we can use these levels to think through our goals and objectives, when and how we want people to practice the skills of peace-keeping, peace-making, and peace-building. For example, consider the writings on mindfulness by noted Vietnamese Buddhist monk, Thich Nhat Hahn (2000), "I think the most important precept of all is to live in awareness, to know what is going on—not only here but there. For instance, when we eat a piece of bread, we may choose to be aware of how our farmers grow the wheat. It seems that chemical poisons are used a bit too much. And while we eat the bread, we are somehow co-responsible for the destruction of our ecology. When we eat a piece of meat, we may become aware that eating meat is not a good way to reconcile oneself with millions of children in the world. Forty thousand children die each day in the Third World for lack of food. And in order to produce meat, you have to feed the cow or the chicken with a lot of cereal.... What we are, what we do every day, has much to do with world peace. If we are aware of our lifestyle, our way of consuming and looking at things, then we know how to make peace right at the present moment. If we are very aware, we will do something to change the course of things" (156).

How do you perceive food differently after reading this passage? Are you ready to respond (i.e., set)? Does this passage provide enough of a guided response for you? If not, what more will you need? Does the concept of mechanism mean that you are so automatic in your eating habits that this kind of mindfulness would take some effort to develop? What complex overt responses would increase your mindfulness about food? What adaptations would allow you to take this mindfulness about food to every meal and snack? What organization would you need in your life to have this mindfulness about food ever present?

136. Use Film for Multi-Sensory Representations of Peace and Reconciliation

In *Teaching and Learning Peace,* Bill Timpson (2002) describes the value he sees in showing sections from the 1982 film, *Gandhi,* as models for peace, reconciliation, and nonviolent conflict resolution. "At a time in history when violence can take on a horrific life of its own, too often escalating into a death struggle of revenge and retaliation, Gandhi's legacy of nonviolent thought and action remain an enduring foundation for the pursuit of peace. Images of British ordered brutality toward unarmed Indian people are juxtaposed throughout the film with Gandhi's own repeated commitment to the moral high ground of nonviolent non-cooperation. These visual and auditory memories seem to last, much more than print, and can serve as competing images to what we have all seen on television of the high-jacked airliners hitting New York's World Trade Center" (114).

Working in Belfast, Northern Ireland in the summer of 2008, Timpson interviewed a youth worker, Dave Magee, who was using the exact same scenes from this film to illustrate the alternatives to retaliation to which Gandhi and his followers were committed. Magee's audiences included former and current members of loyalist paramilitary groups who were quick to say that they never heard about these events in India or these alternatives to violence, but that they could see the relevance to their own situation. "Why were we never told about these before?" they asked.

Watch this now classic film and list the new insights you get into the role of nonviolence, peace, and reconciliation. Identify particular scenes and show them to others to spark a discussion about alternatives to retaliation.

137. Include Diverse Voices and Social Action

In his book chapter, "Approaches to Multicultural Curriculum Reform," James Banks (2001) articulates and critiques common approaches to multicultural curriculum reform and advocates for transformation and social action approaches—deeper approaches that include "reconsidering the goals, structure, and nature of the curriculum" as well as adding non-mainstream, diverse voices, and experiential, socially engaged, and transformative learning to help resolve social problems (240-241). These mechanisms for integrating multicultural content are summarized below:

1. Contributions Approach: Heroes, cultural components, holidays, and other discrete elements related to ethnic groups are added to the curriculum on special days, occasions, and celebrations.

2. Additive Approach: This approach consists of the addition of content, concepts, and themes, and perspectives to the curriculum without changing its structure.

3. Transformation Approach: The basic goals, structure, and nature of the curriculum are changed to enable students to view concepts, events, issues, problems, and themes from the perspectives of diverse cultural, ethnic, and racial groups.

4. Social Action Approach: In this approach, students identify important social problems and issues, gather pertinent data, clarify their values on the issues, make decisions, and take reflective actions to help resolve the issue or problem (240-241).

Analyze your school or organization's current approach to diversity or multicultural content integration. Decide if you want to move toward a deeper approach that goes beyond the contributions and additive approaches. How can this work extend into peacemaking and reconciliation?

138. Transform the Canon

Philosopher Jane Kneller (2003) writes about the challenges she has faced in transforming her courses to include more diverse voices without sacrificing the core of the canon of philosophy that traditionally has comprised her field. The same challenges face anyone teaching about peace and reconciliation —how to include the seminal figures of the field while continuing to explore what new voices might add.

Kneller writes: "As for the problem of squeezing more content into a crowded course, I am still struggling, and no doubt always will, to justify every paragraph I choose to have [students] read, knowing that it means cutting out some other text from an era that deserves a year-long class to cover. . . . For that matter, if we are doing our jobs properly, it can only get worse. The more we research other historical periods, the more material we will find that needs to be added to the canon or forces us to rethink what is canonical in the first place. Indeed, something would be wrong if, over time, it did *not* get harder to teach all this material in one semester. In this respect, good scholarship, be it feminist, multicultural, or other, will always make our task as teachers more challenging" (225).

Re-examine the content of your teachings or learning about peace and reconciliation. What new could be added? Explored? What old could be taken out? Know that this process will help drive your understanding of the field deeper.

STUDYING CHANGE & TAKING INITIATIVE FOR PEACE & RECONCILIATION

Learn about action research and get involved in your community. The word "change" came up big in the Democratic Primaries in 2008 as Barack Obama trumpeted what was needed to end the Iraq War, heal the country, repair the economy, refashion the health care system, and rethink government's fundamental role. Hillary Clinton's early emphasis on "experience" soon morphed into the "candidate who has made changes." Meanwhile, McCain also picked up on change in an effort to distance himself from what the Democrats were calling the "failed policies of the Bush Administration." Scholars of change—Seymour Sarason and Michael Fullan are two of the most cited in educational circles—seem to agree that to be successful, people need to understand the dynamics of change, where and how it can be derailed, and where and how to focus energies and talents.

You can also study the lessons of history—how people fostered change. With respect to peace and reconciliation, we think of Mahatma Gandhi, Nelson Mandela, Betty Reardon, Ada Deer, Elise Boulding, Martin Luther King, Jr., Cesar Chavez, Rosa Parks, Lech Walesa, Leslie Marmon Silko, Leonard Peltier, Rudolfo Anaya, Langston Hughes, Derrick Bell, W.E.B. Du Bois, Maya Angelou, bell hooks, Patricia Hill Collins, Chief Seattle, Wilma Mankiller, Manuelito, and Eleanor Roosevelt. Who would you add to this list? We can respect objectivity and balance but insist on progress, on constructive and nonviolent change.

139. Look Locally and Take Action

Read the local newspapers and check your city's websites for programs and groups to join that are addressing conflict, reconciliation, and peacemaking. In business, government, and nonprofit agencies, we can see the same issues and needs. In *The Third Side,* Bill Ury (1999) notes that within "many organizations, facilitators are working with cross-functional teams to overcome interdepartmental issues. Managers are learning to mediate among their teammates, their employees, and often their multiple bosses. The success of a company is coming to depend on the ability of its people to resolve the innumerable conflicts that crop up between manufacturing and marketing, sales and headquarters, employees and supervisors, and to seek a 'triple win'—a solution good for each side and for the company as a whole" (10).

Look for opportunities to get involved, learn some new skills, and make a difference. For example, some communities have active restorative justice programs where volunteers are welcomed. Various boards and commissions will routinely surface contentious issues that would benefit from some understanding of the principles of mediation. Faith-based groups are often found working with the less fortunate and raising difficult questions about the inequities that exist. Your business or organization may need to address conflicts or tensions. Ask for some discussion about these issues, volunteer to get something started, or invite in someone else with mediation skills.

140. Provide a Suitcase of Hope

To reconcile with a difficult or violent past, creative initiative can make a difference. A new community service project, *Just in Case,* was created and inspired by local artists in Loveland, Colorado, to support young people reconciling with trauma and difficulties in their lives while making the transition to a foster care home. The recycled suitcases are colorful and whimsical, and send hope to confused children in a time of need, often replacing the garbage bags that would otherwise be used for transporting their few personal possessions. To further encourage these kids to find healthy ways to express their feelings, local artists fill each suitcase with writing or drawing journals and a new stuffed toy (*The Healing Path,* March/April, 2008).

Meredith Laine is an experienced college business teacher who was driving down a street in Loveland when she noticed two children sitting on a couch near the road. "They were somewhere in the 8 to 10 year old range. Other items were stacked around them—mattresses, small furniture items, and odds and ends of personal belongings. It took a few minutes for me to process this scene. Then I realized what had happened. The time of day was around 3:30 PM. These children had probably just come from school only to find themselves locked out of their home, and all their worldly possessions placed out on the curb, probably from a foreclosure. There were no adults around; perhaps they were still at work. I found this very disturbing, but then read about the *Just in Case* Program for foster kids.

"Recently a realtor informed me that each week in Colorado in 2007, 1000 mortgages were foreclosed. A tough time for adults, but even harder for kids. Banks and lenders know who occupy their properties and if children are involved. Some governmental agency or non-profit organization could work with these lenders of foreclosed properties and provide a *Suitcase of Hope* to children who are displaced from their homes. A case filled with items to heal; a case for their belongings; a way to show that someone cares and understands. I mean, it shouldn't just always be about money, should it?"

Identify organizations in your community that provide some kind of *Suitcase of Hope*. How could these provide some comfort for the victims of conflict or violence? What *Suitcases* need to be created?

141. Design a Peace Park

The Peace Park in Hiroshima, Japan, is at ground zero for the atom bomb that was dropped in 1945 by the United States. Japanese of all ages make frequent pilgrimages to remember and recommit to nonviolence. Children come from all over Japan to bring their colorful chains of paper cranes, folded with a mindfulness about all those factors that promote peace—cross-cultural understanding, communication, cooperation, sensitivity, empathy, compassion, humility, emotional intelligence, critical and creative thinking.

Take your students to a place on your campus, near your school or in your community that could help raise awareness among visitors about the importance of peace and reconciliation. Develop some recommendations, for example, for a bench with quotations about peace and an invitation to sit and reflect; for a peace pole with local languages expressing "Peace on Earth;" for plaques with images and quotations from the world's great peacemakers; for artwork that was dedicated to peace; for landscaping that is "at peace with the planet and the local bioregion" along with interpretive signage; or for a labyrinth that encourages a walking meditation. What existing spaces could you use "as is" for meditation, vigils, and other gatherings for peace?

142. Help People Face the Reality of Violence and War

During war and its aftermath, there is always a need for healing, both physically and emotionally, for individuals, their communities, and nations. One essential step is to look honestly at all the repercussions of violence, no matter how troubling or sensitive the issue. While the calls to "Support Our Troops" were repeated regularly at rallies and in editorials, it is not clear what the implications are for this kind of appeal when "our troops" are involved in violations of the Geneva Convention or violence back home, for example.

Emphasize that sophisticated communication skills and high levels of emotional intelligence can help in processing information like what appears in an article for *The New York Times* on January 13, 2008. According to authors Sontag and Alvarez, there were 121 cases in which veterans of Iraq and Afghanistan committed a killing in this country, or were charged with one, after their return from war. In many of those cases, combat trauma and the stress of deployment—along with a range of other problems including alcohol abuse and family troubles—contributed to these tragedies. Volatile emotions then mix with violence and self-destructive tendencies to produce an explosive, deadly concoction. Three-quarters of these veterans were still in the military at the time of the killing. More than half the killings involved guns, and the rest were stabbings, beatings, strangulations, and bathtub drownings. Twenty-five offenders faced murder, manslaughter, or homicide charges for fatal car crashes resulting from drunken, reckless, or suicidal driving.

According to Sontag and Alvarez, about a third of the victims were spouses, girlfriends, children, or other relatives, among them 2-year-old Krisiauna Calaira Lewis, whose 20-year-old father slammed her against a wall when he was recuperating in Texas from a bombing near Falluja that blew off his foot and shook up his brain. A quarter of the victims were fellow service members, including Specialist Richard Davis of the Army, who was stabbed repeatedly and then set ablaze, his body hidden in the woods by fellow soldiers a day after they all returned from Iraq. And the rest were acquaintances or strangers, among them Noah P. Gamez, 21, who was breaking into a car at a Tucson motel when an Iraq combat veteran, also 21, caught him, shot him dead, and then killed himself outside San Diego with one of several guns found in his car.

Add to this the alarming number of suicides among enlisted and returning veterans. According to the *Times On-Line* for October 3, 2008, "More American military veterans have been committing suicide than US soldiers have been dying in Iraq. . . . At least 6,256 US veterans took their lives in 2005, at an average of 17 a day, according to figures broadcast last night. Former servicemen are more than twice as likely as the rest of the population to commit suicide. Such statistics compare to the total of 3,863 American military deaths in Iraq since the invasion in 2003—an average of 2.4 a day, according to the website Icasualties. org. The rate of suicides among veterans prompted claims that the US was suffering from a 'mental health epidemic'—often linked to post-traumatic stress."

Note how troubling it is to read the graphic details about the human stories that underlie the statistics. It is no surprise that the proponents of a particular war do not like to see these kinds of statistics or details made public. Yet it is in the public arena that democracy must play out. Take time to prepare an audience, to set ground rules for discussion, and to debrief the process when completed.

143. Take a Public Stand on Peace and Reconciliation

History has noted when communities, large and small, have turned against war and demanded a return to peace. The end of the Vietnam War, for example, was hastened by demonstrations and marches that grew in number and intensity. Most communities also have options for speaking before elected officials. In Fort Collins, Colorado, the City Council allows thirty minutes before the formal meeting begins for citizen comments of any nature. From 2007 through 2008, a group of peace activists surfaced a resolution that called for an end of funding for the U.S. War in Iraq, for American troops to come home, and for full funding of the medical support they will need. On different occasions, citizens were invited to speak to this resolution and encourage members of City Council to follow what many other cities had done and formally vote their support. These kinds of opportunities allow anyone to extend discussion into the public arena. These kinds of formats also force speakers to be concise, thoughtful, and appropriate in their comments, always a useful exercise when "teaching peace and reconciliation."

Stephanie King was completing her doctoral studies for a career in ministry education when she wrote this: "I attended a church service that was all on human trafficking and what we can do to assist those sold into it. This was a very powerful and moving service that ignited a passion in me to do something about this situation."

Invite speakers from religious organizations or community groups to talk about what they are doing to better society and work towards peace.

144. Become a Servant Leader for Peace and Reconciliation

The change needed to create a culture of peace and care in schools requires a transformation in leadership. Service leadership offers a basis for such transformative leadership because it is based on the idea of connectedness and participation. In this way service is seen as "any action that is other-oriented" (Inouye, *et al.* 2006, 206). Project Service Leadership (PSL), for example, assists Pacific Northwest school districts in integrating service-learning into their curriculum. According to their website, "It has helped thousands of Northwest teachers, schools, and colleges of education to enrich their instructional effectiveness through service-learning initiatives by providing staff training, teacher institutes, phone consultation, program development assistance, and resource materials. (See: www.projectserviceleadership.org/)

In essence, service learning has meant that teachers link course content to meaningful service activities, usually off campus. For example, in Bill Timpson's university Honors seminar on peacemaking, students choose from a number of different agencies where they can volunteer fifteen hours of time and effort during the semester. In the past, some have worked with the restorative justice program in the city or at Ten Thousand Villages, a Mennonite nonprofit store that is dedicated to fair trade practices with artists in developing nations. At the end of the semester, these students then complete a report of their experiences, the connections they saw with their readings, and how these experiences impacted their understanding of peacemaking.

If a school adopts a service learning or leadership framework, everyone is theoretically better able to live out the moral values of honesty, respect, responsibility, fairness, and compassion as shared core values among the groups of people who comprise the larger school community. Such a school community can help create positive energy and collective happiness among its members.

As educators and people interested in education, we can ask ourselves how we can adopt a program of service leadership and learning for our schools, colleges, and universities.

145. Study Connectedness and Promote Peaceful Change

We can choose to create a new story for our schools, an alternative and peaceful story. This story represents a discourse—a way of thinking, believing, and acting. It is an alternative story to the dominant or traditional story of schooling in many parts of the western world. Because it is an alternative story, it offers each of us choices. We will be left to choose among stories or discourses we want to listen to and follow. We will no longer be tied to one traditional story about the status quo.

The theme of this new discourse is change. We can deliberately use the word "change" rather than "reform" because reform is normally interpreted as modification or revision of the status quo. Commonly schools talk about reform. In contrast to change, reform is about making minor adjustments to the status quo. The emphasis is on replacing or repairing parts of the school. Whereas, change, particularly profound change, involves setting aside our assumptions and mindsets, and becoming open to new realities—both individually and collectively, so that together we can create a new future.

From the new sciences such as quantum physics and chaos theory (Wheatley 1999), we know that the key principle for this kind of change is connectedness (Senge et al. 2005). And the focus here is on the connectedness or relationships among people, particularly the people who make up our school and higher education communities—students, teachers, parents, administrators, staff, and the wider local community. What are ways in which we can create a new discourse of connectedness in our schools, colleges, universities, and lives that promotes peace and reconciliation?

146. Make Continuous Improvement toward Peace and Reconciliation

Working towards peace and reconciliation means ongoing efforts—daily, weekly, monthly, annually—on many fronts—political, social, economic, cultural, psychological, behavioral, and more. Jen Fullerton has extensive experience in Human Resource Development and has seen the concept of "Emotional Intelligence" grow in popularity in the corporate field as organizations make efforts to develop more effective communication among employees and help them resolve conflicts and tensions in constructive, sustainable ways. She writes about her frustrations when the benefits of training too often disappeared without follow-up. "A consultant conducted a workshop in an organization where I formerly worked. The workshop was excellent. However, it proved to be more of a temporary bonding experience than a real or deep learning experience because the communication tools were quickly forgotten after the workshop. Employees in the division resumed their old habits and little of substance changed."

Fullerton draws an example about workplace conflicts from Deborah Tannen's (1998) *The Argument Culture:* "Women at work frequently express puzzlement at how men can argue with each other and then continue as if nothing happened. In a parallel way, men at work are often surprised when women are deeply upset by a verbal attack—taking personally what the men feel is simply part of getting the job done" (195-196).

Assess your own experiences with workshops or training in conflict resolution, reconciliation, communication, or other aspects of peacemaking. Consider what kinds of follow up would have ensured greater success.

147. Keep on Walking

We can learn much about peace and reconciliation from the study of leaders, both national and community. In his autobiography, *Long Walk to Freedom,* Nelson Mandela describes in detail his life in South Africa, from his boyhood to his active resistance to racial apartheid, the 27 years he spent in prison on Robbin Island, and his leadership in the movement toward democracy that eventually led to his election as President. Yet, Mandela has always been clear about the ongoing challenges that everyone must rise to meet if we are to leave our worlds better than how we found them. "I have walked that long road to freedom. I have tried not to falter; I have made missteps along the way. But I have discovered the secret that after climbing a great hill, one only finds that there are more hills to climb. I have taken a moment here to rest, to steal a view of the glorious vista that surrounds me, to look back on the distance I have come. But I can rest only for a moment, for with freedom comes responsibilities, and I dare not linger, for my long walk is not yet ended" (625).

Take a moment to list several examples of peace and reconciliation that you have seen in your lifetime, whether personal, national, or international. Note what underlies them, what connects them. Identify your role and/or reaction to each. Now look off to the future and identify those challenges that await us all and what paths lay ahead. What will be your role? What actions will you take?

POSTSCRIPT

There is so much to be done to turn people and nations away from the scourge of violence and militarism, and toward the life affirming skills, beliefs, attitudes, actions, and values contained within work on peace and reconciliation. The previous 147 "Tips" address many eternal truths, yet the possibilities for new ideas and initiatives are also infinite. We will need to tap these eternal truths as well as search for new possibilities for transforming the violence in our present world. As Nelson Mandela challenged himself to keep on walking, so must we, individually and collectively, continue moving forward toward that peaceful future. There is no other option. Add your own "Tips" to this discussion and recruit others to do likewise. We'd love to hear from you. You can always contact us through Atwood Publishing or our current University positions.

CONCLUSION

A Synergistic, Trans-disciplinary Scholarship for Teaching Peace and Reconciliation: An International Collaboration

William M. Timpson, Edward J. Brantmeier, Nathalie Kees,
Tom Cavanagh, Claire McGlynn, and Elavie Ndura-Ouédraogo

The teaching of peace and reconciliation is inherently complex, dynamic, and often volatile when debated or discussed. Teaching about sustainability or diversity evokes similar challenges. Instructors who address one or more of these topics can benefit from concise and practical ideas or "Tips" that are pulled from established paradigms as well as from the original thinking of teachers at all levels. What has resulted in this book project is a new compilation of both established theories and original innovations, from scholars, teachers, students, and others.

Drawing on her work on teaching, culture, and communication, for example, bell hooks (2003), underscores the connections between conflict, power, and racism. "When the tragic events of 9/11 occurred, it was as though, in just a few moments in time, all our work to end domination in all its forms, all our pedagogies of hope, were rendered meaningless as much of the American public, reacting to the news coverage of the tragedy, responded with an outpouring of imperialist, white-supremacist, nationalist, capitalist, patriarchal rage against terrorists defined as dark-skinned others, even when there were no images, no concrete proof" (9).

In a similar way, David Orr rips into conventional wisdom about intelligence when environmental devastation and violence are committed by some of the brightest and best educated. In the opening pages of *Earth in Mind,* first published in 1994, yet hauntingly accurate still more than a decade later, he writes: "If today is a typical day on planet earth, we will lose another 72 square miles of rain forest, or about an acre a second....We will lose 40 to 250 species....And today we will add 2,700 tons of chlorofluorocarbons and 15 million tons of carbon dioxide to the atmosphere....The truth is that many things on which our future health and prosperity depend are in dire jeopardy....It is worth noting that this is not the work of ignorant people. Rather, it is largely the results of work by people with BAs, BSs, LLBs, MBAs, and PhDs. Elie Wiesel once made a similar point, noting that the designers and perpetrators of Auschwitz, Dachau, and Buchenwald—the Holocaust—were the heirs of Kant and Goethe, widely thought to be the best educated people on earth" (7).

As scholars, it is our studied belief that teaching the principles and skills of peace and reconciliation can offer constructive and hopeful ways forward, ways to manage conflicts without resorting to violence and build capacity for change, even in the most desperate of times. More specifically, our work on this book has led us to six underlying principles.

First, we have come to discover that teaching peace and reconciliation requires everyone to understand something about the *change process* and have some skill in mediating its expression. Michael Fullan (1991) notes that an openness to change, for example, requires some measure of intellectual and emotional sophistication; i.e., an ability to reflect and rethink, a desire to learn, listen and empathize, to solve problems, negotiate differences, and to work effectively in teams. In one of his more recent works, Fullan (2005) describes those qualities of major educational reform efforts that are enduring and, therefore, sustainable. "The solution will require us to use complexity and systems theory, but in my use of it, every abstract concept must be accompanied by a practical strategy that illustrates the concept in action" (13). As contributors to this book on teaching peace and reconciliation, we had to find concise and practical ways to communicate basic concepts to audiences of varying ages, backgrounds, and interests. Connecting the abstract to the concrete helps us move forward with peaceful solutions that work.

Second, if we are to ask people, young and old, to take on the complexities, ambiguities, and difficulties of the "real world" and to think more deeply about the consequences of conflict and violence, as well as the potential for peace and reconciliation, then we need to establish a *positive climate* in our classes, organizations, and communities. Abraham Maslow (1959) is often cited for addressing this need for trust as a foundation for learning. Several "Tips" for our book utilize cooperative learning and promote trust, for example.

Third, *communication* must be respectful and honest for deeper learning to occur. Students and instructors, indeed every citizen in a democracy, should feel safe to question others, rethink their beliefs, and explore new ideas. As William Perry (1999) has theorized, these processes can be gateways to those higher levels of cognitive processing which give us the skills we need to handle greater degrees of complexity and ambiguity. The complexities surrounding safety, communication, climate, and change, however, are compounded when instructors assume the role of *champions* for conflict resolution, peace, and reconciliation within our institutions. The research on critical thinking, for example, is very clear: we can get better and more creative decisions when we solicit many different viewpoints, if we can handle the attendant challenges of effective communication and group dynamics. In her groundbreaking work on leadership, Meg Wheatley (1999) writes: "(Multiple) and varying responses, [give] a genuine richness to ... observations. An organization rich with many interpretations develops a wiser sense of what is going on and what needs to be done. Such organizations become more intelligent" (67). When we value diversity, we honor, respect, and promote a deeper learning that can foster wisdom in individuals and in groups. Such leadership can help deconstruct the barriers to progress and reconstruct new economic, political, social, and environmental systems.

Fourth, instructors and leaders need to be attentive to those dynamics that stifle exploration and inhibit learning about peace and reconciliation. We must find the time in our content-packed courses, presentations, and agendas to address essential *process* issues, those skills which people need to rethink their own ideas, learning, and development, how effective communication supports group work, and how periods of discussion, reflection, and attention to interpersonal dynamics can promote deeper learning (Timpson 1999). Although unnerving to some, moments of silence in and out of the classroom can be golden.

Fifth, culture is an important consideration when talking about the environment for teaching about peace and reconciliation in schools, colleges, universities, organizations, and communities. As Macfarlane et al. (2007) note, "Creating a culture of care in schools—culturally-safe classrooms and culturally-safe schools—involves challenging and reviewing systemic processes that exist....No one can pretend that getting a consensus on creating culturally-safe schools is a simple task for school administrators and classroom teachers" (73-74). However, the tips offered in this book can point people toward developing practices, policies, and programs that are tailored to their particular contexts and cultures. Some tips move toward deeper cultural relativism— understanding groups and society within situated, contextual histories. Other tips move toward universal, transcendent human values, needs, and connection.

Finally, and given the horrific toll that violence and conflicts of all sorts takes on so many aspects of our lives together on this planet, we must also address fundamental issues of *survival*. In his compelling and historical analysis of societies that faced threats and adapted or collapsed, Jared Diamond (2005) challenges us to study the record of human responses and reflect on what we face today. Survival for humans and the planet is not an abstract or lofty area of study, but a day to day reality that should guide our choices as individuals, societies, nation-states, and global citizens. Violence only serves to undermine survival; peace and reconciliation move us forward.

WORKING TOGETHER

At the beginning, the contributors to earlier books of "Tips" for teaching diversity and sustainability spent much time discussing core issues and defining terms. We now know better how important language becomes when addressing complex and sensitive issues. Jerome Bruner (1966), for example, spent much of his career demonstrating the power in conceptual learning for providing a framework for a deeper understanding. With respect to teaching peace and reconciliation, we spent time early on exploring existing definitions, discussing concepts and how our understanding of the teaching of diversity and sustainability might apply.

For our work on teaching peace and reconciliation, the editors pooled expertise and experiences, building on a broad base of core readings including some that we all knew and others that drew more on particular disciplinary expertise in teacher education, educational psychology, counseling, philosophy, and restorative practices. The literature on postsecondary instruction is rich and growing (e.g., Davis 1993; Eble 1994; Lowman 2000; Timpson 1999; Timpson and Bourgogne 2002; McKeachie and Svinicki 2006; Timpson and Doe 2008). We now understand better what we need as instructors, presenters, and leaders to effectively address complex and contentious issues in our own classes.

Contributors to our peace and reconciliation project built on their relationships on campus and through AERA's Special Interest Group (SIG) on Peace Education. As specific "Tips" were developed, they were shared via email among the six editors. Bill Timpson and Ed Brantmeier took the lead and others contributed as time and opportunity permitted. In 2008, Timpson also journeyed to Queen's University in Belfast, Northern Ireland, to work directly with Claire McGlynn and her colleagues.

In order to track progress and address concerns—the accountability component of our synergistic collaboration, if you will—we also created a survey for contributors to reflect on their involvement in this project. We asked each editor and contributor to respond to the following prompts:

- It is important for peace educators to pool their talents and expertise and *collaborate* on new and original works of scholarship.

- By drawing teachers and scholars together, out of their isolation from each other, contributors to a collaborative project like this book can tap into an exciting and productive *synergy* when the whole is greater than the sum of its individual parts.

- Collaborating with other peace educators can be a *creative challenge*.

- Interacting with others to produce a new work of scholarship helps contributors to *deepen* their own understanding.

- Working *deductively*—reasoning from the general or theoretical to the specific—allows contributors to tap the existing body of work on peace education.

- Working *inductively*—seeing new ideas emerge from applications, trials, exploration—allows the editors to see new possibilities for diverse contributors.

In this project on teaching peace and reconciliation, we saw parallels to previous work on teaching diversity and teaching sustainability, and various themes below emerged from the interactions and responses of editors and contributors.

Theme 1: Sharing Ideas

When assessing these projects and their impact on synergistic collaboration, it has proven helpful to understand the individual authors' experiences with sharing their writing: "Having others share and present their writing kept me focused and on task to write myself." "[This was an] energizing project. I enjoyed co-writing the chapter .... It made me focus on aspects of my teaching and the philosophical approach I was actually using." Another contributor wrote, "One truly recognizes the value of sharing ideas; it multiplies energies in ways that urge the individual to contribute positively to the whole." Another affirmed, "It has been very refreshing, at this point in my career, to find other like-minded colleagues to collaborate with."

Theme 2: Reflections about Teaching

The synergy that resulted from collaboration on these projects was sparked, in part, by each instructor's thinking about teaching, an outcome that is especially significant at a research university where the pressures to publish can be enormous: "[This project] has made me reflect on various issues, i.e., the curriculum, my choice of texts and readings, my teaching, and my interactions with students." Another contributor relays, "This project helped provide the courage for me to mainstream more peace and reconciliation approaches in my teacher education and educational leadership courses."

For teaching diversity, several contributors also wrote about issues of safety when addressing difficult and sensitive issues, both for students and themselves, something equally of concern for those teaching about peace and reconciliation. One respondent to our survey returned to that theme when commenting on the need for reflection: "[This project] made me think about what our role is in challenging students in their beliefs and prejudices while creating an accepting environment in which all opinions are allowed a voice." Several contributors also remarked on their increased sensitivity to the issues: "I seek more sharing of in-depth personal stories from the students." A number of respondents remarked on their increased sensitivity to the needs of specific populations: "More time is now spent thinking and talking about the interaction between education and social class privilege." One added, "I have learned a great deal about the different types of peace education, including restorative justice and violence reduction. Taking many of the people, concepts, and theories that I share in my counseling classes and writing them up in brief teaching techniques was a helpful practice for me. I enjoy putting what I do in the classroom on paper."

Theme 3: Connecting Teaching and Research

The opportunity for collaborators to reflect on these three projects raised other related issues and questions: "The lack of wider interest on campus reinforces the perception that teaching is truly undervalued at a research university, and this one, in particular." "The scholarship of teaching can bridge the domains of research and teaching." For those working on "Tips" for teaching peace and reconciliation, several positives emerged. The three contributing editors at Colorado State University met regularly. What one person developed and trialed with students, encouraged and inspired the others. A real multiplier effect emerged. Moreover, their discussions invariably moved from the theoretical to the practical as results were shared and analyzed. As important, their shared interest in teaching found expression in their work on this project of original scholarship. Comments from the other editors on various "Tips" as they were shared provided valuable feedback, especially when they could reference their experiences in other cultures, i.e., Northern Ireland, Burundi, the Maori in New Zealand. One contributor added, "It was nice to see that concepts and practices from the field of psychology and counseling are being used within teacher education as well as peace education. I was glad that I could add some considerations from the counseling field on how to best conduct some of these activities, how to find original sources for some of the concepts, and how to improve on questioning techniques for processing activities."

Theme 4: Speaking Truth to Power

According to H. Larry Ingle, a Quaker who taught history at the University of Tennessee, the phrase "speaking truth to power" goes back to 1955, when the American Friends Service Committee published *Speak Truth to Power,* a pamphlet that offered a new approach to the Cold War. For those working on "Tips" for teaching peace and reconciliation, some challenges emerged about the place for this work in light of conventional "state standards" for teacher education in the U.S. However, contributors took heart, for example, from what our colleagues were doing in Northern Ireland's integrated schools to refashion the curricula and help that deeply divided society emerge from centuries of violence.

In a parallel manner, those writing about teaching diversity and sustainability often confront entrenched beliefs and attitudes that oppose change. For example, contributors to *Teaching Sustainability* felt that the project's ambitious scope was both intimidating and energizing. One contributor wrote: "The issue of sustainability is so big and complex that the very idea of a concise book of practical tips for teaching it seems, at first glance, impossible, naïve, overly simplistic. Yet we all came to believe that, done well, this book could be a valuable contribution to anyone concerned about waste and pollution; energy conservation, consumption, truths about Earth's finite resources and energy capacity, and the reality of population growth and ever increasing demands for production." For the *Teaching Diversity* project, the openness and honesty among the contributors allowed them to raise issues of safety, at least among themselves, as they challenged the university's public rhetoric about its value for inclusiveness.

Theme 5: The Benefits and Challenges of Synergy

Clearly, this experience whetted the contributors' appetites for similar projects. Instead of the commonly heard concerns about the time required, what emerged more often were ideas for more and different conversations and activities, including how best to interface with the university, the schools, and surrounding community: "Secure university support, resources, leadership, etc., if possible, so as to capture the synergy of faculty and staff on campus working on a topic of significant importance to the university." While synergy is a complex and elusive construct to make real, here was real evidence of its expression. Another noted, "I definitely think the outcome of this project is greater than any of us could have done individually. I really appreciated being able to acknowledge people who have contributed to my classes over the years." The challenge would be in sustaining these interactions once the writing projects were completed.

CONCLUSIONS FROM THE EDITORS

In many ways, the writing of this book on peace and reconciliation has sparked new, stimulating, and productive interactions among university faculty, staff, and students (who are otherwise isolated from each other) and interested colleagues in the schools and larger community. The emphasis on the scholarship of teaching has been especially beneficial when the discussion of promising instructional practices is elevated to a more rigorous, research-based level and contributors can be given credit for their innovations and efforts. Stepping back, we can also see clearly how peace and reconciliation connects with work on teaching diversity and sustainability—four of the most compelling issues facing humans in the twenty-first century.

These issues play out in different ways in different contexts. For example, at universities, we have general agreement about what constitutes research, i.e., peer-reviewed publications and grants, chapters and books of original scholarship. However, we are much less certain about what constitutes quality instruction. Course design is one aspect, as is effective delivery, i.e., instructor knowledge, preparation, and organization. A focus on deeper student learning, however—application, analysis, synthesis, and evaluation—introduces other degrees of complexity. The focus on peace and reconciliation, diversity, and sustainability adds yet more layers.

Accordingly, we want to argue for more substantive investment in professional development in schools, colleges, and universities, but also in any business, organization, or group wanting to build its capacity for change. Here we want to make an argument that the benefits of action learning, peer coaching, mentoring, videotape analysis, mid-semester student feedback, and the like are promising (e.g., Timpson and Broadbent 1995; Timpson and Doe 2008). Because the nature of peace and reconciliation involves so many facets—e.g., conflict management, collaboration, communication, mediation, negotiation, remembering and forgiveness, unlearning hatred, valuing differences—we must be aware of the need for active exploration to reexamine values and beliefs in the light of new information and competing ideas. Thomas Kuhn's (1970) groundbreaking work on paradigm shifts has been a constant reference for us, both for questions about professional development and student learning.

Change in higher education—or any institution, for that matter—will not come quickly or easily. Accordingly, we believe that special funds should be provided to encourage new conversations, the sharing of ideas and new course designs and deliveries, and the extension of work by scholars into the larger community. For example, Bill Timpson and Fiona Broadbent's (1995) work with the *Action Learning Project* at the University of Queensland documents the benefits when real resources are attached to a systematic university effort at change. We also want to argue for institutional support for new and original research on topics related to teaching peace and reconciliation. For example, in a report for the Carnegie Foundation for the Advancement of Teaching, Shirley Kenney (1998) argues that much can be done to reinvigorate undergraduate education if universities did more to connect their research priorities with instruction.

While individuals can contribute important insights and examples, leadership is also needed to expand these benefits across an organization. The cases we have featured and explored in these projects involve complex, interdependent issues that defy easy answers. Our thinking and responses, then, must be correspondingly sophisticated and creative, sensitive to nuances and competing values, truly interdisciplinary at a time when so many forces push us to abdicate to highly specialized experts.

Addressing the challenges of teaching about peace and reconciliation with all their inherent challenges puts a premium on effective communication skills. Unfortunately, within traditional paradigms of instruction and their focus on content coverage, precious little time is available for attention to those process skills that can deepen learning. For example, Joseph Lowman (2000) argues for the centrality of relationships and enthusiasm for increasing engagement and learning. We agree. Teaching about peace and reconciliation will build from a solid understanding of basic concepts. However, for a deeper learning to result, we will also need those process skills of reflective listening, empathy, consensus, negotiation, and cooperation.

As an editorial team, we want to support you the reader as you teach about peace and reconciliation at work and at play, out in the community, and at home. We also invite you to engage with us and the ideas we share in this book. Take some chances. Explore new ideas and approaches. Contribute to our efforts to defuse violence in our world.

REFERENCES & RESOURCES

——— . 2000. *A Force More Powerful.* Film. Producers Steve York and Miriam A. Zimmerman. Washington DC: WETA. Http://www.aforcemorepowerful.org/index.php.

14th Dalai Lama. 1999. *Ethics for the new millennium.* New York: Riverhead Books.

Allport, Gordon. 1954. *The nature of prejudice.* Cambridge, MA: Addison-Wesley.

Anglin, James. 2003. *Pain, normality, and the struggle for congruence: Reinterpreting residential care for children and youth.* New York: Haworth Press.

Apter, Joan. 1994. *Council facilitator's guidebook for sixth grade.* Ojai, CA: The Ojai Foundation.

Artress, Lauren. 2006. *Walking a sacred path: Rediscovering the labyrinth as a spiritual practice.* New York: Penguin Group, Inc.

Ausubel, David. 1963. *The psychology of meaningful verbal learning: An introduction to school learning.* New York: Grune and Stratton.

Azar, Edward, Paul Jureidini, and Ronald McLaurin. 1978. Protracted social conflict. *Theory and Practice in the Middle East Journal of Palestine Studies.* 8 (1): 41-60.

Bajaj, Monisha. 2008. 'Critical' Peace Education. In *Encyclopedia of peace education*, ed. Monisha Bajaj. Charlotte, North Carolina: Information Age Publishing, 135-144.

Banks, James A. 2007. Approaches to multicultural curriculum reform. In *Multicultural education: Issues and perspectives*, 6th ed., eds. James A. Banks and Cherry A. McGee Banks. Hoboken, NJ: Wiley & Son, 247-267.

———. 2008. Diversity, group identity, and citizenship education in a global age. *Educational Researcher.* 37 (3): 129-139.

Banning, James. 2003. The institution's commitment to diversity. In *Teaching diversity*, eds. William M. Timpson, Silvia Canetto, Evelinn Borrayo, and Ray Yang, 207-216. Madison, WI: Atwood Publishing.

Bekerman, Zvi and Claire McGlynn, eds. 2007. *Addressing ethnic conflict through peace education: International perspectives.* New York: Palgrave Macmillan.

Bekerman, Zvi, Michalinos Zembylas, and Claire McGlynn. 2008. Working towards the de-essentialization of identity categories in conflict and post-conflict societies: Israel, Cyprus, and Northern Ireland. Paper presented at the annual meeting for the International Association for Intercultural Education, June 30-July 3, Warsaw, Poland.

————. 2009. Challenging identity essentialization in conflict and post-conflict societies: Israel, Cyprus, and Northern Ireland. In *Theory and Practice in Intercultural Education*, eds. Krystyna Bleszynska, Jagdish Gundara, and Agostino Portera.

Bennett, Milton J. 1979. Overcoming the golden rule: Sympathy and empathy. In *Communication Yearbook* 3, ed. Dan Nimmo, 407-422. Beverly Hills, CA: Sage.

Bennett, Milton J. 1998. Overcoming the golden rule: Sympathy and empathy. In *Basic concepts of intercultural communication*, ed. Milton J. Bennett, 191-214. Yarmouth, Maine: Intercultural Press.

Berrigan, Daniel. 2000. Connecting the altar to the pentagon. In *Peace is the way*, ed. Walter Wink. Maryknoll, NY: Orbis Books, 93-97.

Bishop, Russell. 2005. Freeing ourselves from neocolonial domination in research: A kaupapa Maori approach to creating knowledge. In *The Sage handbook of qualitative research*, 3rd ed., eds. Norman K. Denzin and Yvonna S. Lincoln, 109-138. Thousand Oaks, CA: Sage.

Bishop, Russell, and Mere Berryman. 2006. *Culture speaks: Cultural relationships and classroom learning*. Wellington, New Zealand: Huia.

Bloom, Benjamin, Max Engelhart, Edward Furst, Walker Hill, and David Krathwohl. 1956. *Taxonomy of educational objectives, Handbook I: Cognitive domain*. New York: Longman Green.

Bloom, Benjamin S. 1973. *Every kid can: Learning for mastery*. Washington, DC: College University Press.

Boal, Augosto. 1979. *Theater of the oppressed*. New York: Arisen.

————. 1992. *Games for actors and non-actors*. New York: Routledge.

————. 1995. *Rainbow of desire*. New York: Routledge.

Bohm, David, and Lee Nichol. 1986. *On dialogue*. New York: Routledge.

Boulding, Elise. 2000. *Cultures of peace: The hidden side of history*. New York: Syracuse University Press.

Boyd, James. 2003. Teaching the diversity of world religions. In *Teaching diversity*, eds. William M. Timpson, Silvia Canetto, Evelinn Borrayo, and Ray Yang, 65-75. Madison, WI: Atwood Publishing.

Brantmeier, Edward J. 2003. Self education for an interdependent world: Core concepts for creating globalized teachers. CD-ROM. UNESCO Conference on Intercultural Education Conference Proceedings, eds. Johanna Lasonen and Leena Lestinen. University of Jyvaskyla, Finland: Institute of Educational Research.

————. 2007. Everyday understandings of peace and non-peace: Peacekeeping and peacebuilding at a U.S. Midwestern high school. *Journal of Peace Education*, 4 (2): 127-148.

————. 2007. Connecting Inner and Outer Peace: Buddhist Meditation Integrated with Peace Education. *Infactis Pax*. 1 (2): 120-157. Also available at www.infactispax. org/journal/

————. 2008. Building empathy for intercultural peace: Teacher involvement in peace curricula development at a U.S. Midwestern High School. In *Transforming educa-*

tion for peace, eds. Jing Lin, Edward Brantmeier, and Christa Bruhn. Greenwich, CT: Information Age Publishing.

Brantmeier, Edward, and Jing Lin. 2008. Introduction: Toward forging a positive, transformative paradigm for peace education. In *Transforming education for peace*, eds. Jing Lin, Edward Brantmeier, and Christa Bruhn, xiii-xviii. Greenwich, CT: Information Age Publishing.

Brendtro, Larry. 2006. Kids in pain. In *Resilience revolution: Discovering strengths in challenging kids*, ed. Larry K. Brendtro, 3-30. Bloomington, IN: Solution Tree.

Brown, John S. and Richard P. Adler. 2008. Minds on Fire: Open Education, the Long Tail, and Learning 2.0. *Educause Review*. 43 (1):16-32.

Brown, Rexford. 1991. *Schools of thought: How the politics of literacy shape thinking in the classroom*. San Francisco: Jossey-Bass.

Brumbeau, Jeff, and Gail de Marcken. 2000. *The quiltmaker's gift*. New York: Scholastic.

Bruner, Jerome. 1966. *Toward a theory of instruction*. Cambridge, MA: Harvard University Press.

Bubar, Roe, and Irene Vernon. 2003. A Native perspective on teaching law and U.S. policy. In *Teaching diversity*, eds. William M. Timpson, Silvia Canetto, Evelinn Borrayo, and Ray Yang, 153-168. Madison, WI: Atwood Publishing.

Canetto, Silvia, and Evelinn Borrayo. 2003. Alien perspectives in accented voices: Classroom dynamics when international female instructors teach diversity content. In *Teaching diversity*, eds. William M. Timpson, Silvia Canetto, Evelinn Borrayo, and Ray Yang, 189-205. Madison, WI: Atwood Publishing.

Capra, Fritjof. 1999. The web of life: A new scientific understanding of living systems. New York: Anchor Books, Doubleday.

Carroll, John. 1963. A model of school learning. *Teachers College Record*, 64, 723-733.

Cavanagh, Thomas. 2007. Focusing on relationships creates safety in schools. *Research Information for Teachers*. 1: 31-35.

———. 2008a. Schooling for happiness: Rethinking the aims of education. *Kairaranga*, 9 (1): 20-23.

———. 2008b. *Schooling for peaceful relationships: Advancing the theory of a culture of care*. Paper presented at the American Educational Research Association (AERA), New York City.

Chodron, Pema. 1994. *Start where you are: A guide to compassionate living*. Boston, MA: Shambhala Publications.

———. 2001. *Tonglen: The path of transformation*. Halifax, Nova Scotia: Vajradhatu Publications.

Christie, Nils. 1977. Conflicts as property. *British Journal of Criminology*, 17 (1): 1-15.

Conze, Edward. 1956. *Buddhist meditation*. London: George Allen and Unwin LTD.

Covey, Steven. 1989. *The seven habits of highly effective people*. New York: Simon and Schuster.

Danesh, Hossian B. 2006. Toward an integrative theory of peace education. *Journal of Peace Education*, 3 (1): 55-78.

Davies, Lyn. 2004. *Education and conflict: Complexity and chaos.* London: Routledge Falmer.

Davis, Barbara. 1993. *Tools for teaching.* San Francisco: Jossey-Bass.

Deloria, Vine, and Daniel Wildcat. 2001. *Power and place: Indian education in America.* Golden, CO: Fulcrum Publishing.

Devi, Nischala J. 1994. *Dynamic stillness #2: On dynamic stillness meditation guidance.* CD. Fairfax, CA.

Diamond, Jared. 2005. *Collapse: How societies choose to fail or succeed.* New York: Viking.

Dinur, Esty. 2006. In *Long shadows: Veterans' paths to peace,* ed. David Giffey, 235-250. Madison, WI: Atwood Publishing.

Douglass, Frederick. 1855. *My bondage and my freedom.* New York and Auburn: Miller, Orton, and Mulligan.

Dreikurs, Rudolph. 1968. *Psychology in the classroom.* New York: Harper and Row.

Duarte, Eduardo, and Stacy Smith. 2000. *Foundational perspectives in multicultural education.* New York: Longman.

Eble, Kenneth. 1994. *The craft of teaching.* San Francisco: Jossey-Bass

Friedman, Maurice. 2000. Hasidism and the love of enemies. In *Peace is the way*, Walter Wink, ed. 118-123. Maryknoll, NY: Orbis Books.

Freire, Paulo. 1970. *Pedagogy of the oppressed.* London: Penguin Books.

Fullan, Michael. 1991. *The new meaning of educational change.* New York: Teacher's College Press.

———. 2001. *Leading in a culture of change.* Thousand Oaks, CA: Corwin.

———. 2005. *Leadership and sustainability.* Thousand Oaks, CA: Corwin.

Galtung, Johan. 1969. Violence, peace, and peace research. *Journal of Peace Research*, 3: 167-192.

———. 1988. *Peace and social structure: Essays in peace research.* Copenhagen: Christian Eljers.

Galtung, Johan, and Carl Jacobsen. 2000. *Peace by peaceful means.* Thousand Oaks, CA: Sage.

Gandhi, Arun. 2003. *Legacy of love: My education in the path of nonviolence.* El Sobrante, California: North Bay Books.

Gandhi, Mohandas K. 1924. Young India. In *Collected works of Mahatma Gandhi (May-August 1924).* 25: 390.

Garb, Joel. 2006. In *Long shadows: Veterans' paths to peace,* ed. David Giffey, 181-192. Madison, WI: Atwood Publishing.

Gardner, Howard. 1983. *Frames of mind.* New York: Basic Books.

———. 1999a. *The disciplined mind: What all students should understand.* New York: Simon and Schuster.

———. 1999b. *Intelligence reframed: Multiple intelligences for the 21ist century.* New York: Basic Books.

Giffey, David, ed. 2006. *Long shadows: Veterans' paths to peace.* Madison, WI: Atwood Publishing.

Goleman, Daniel. 1994. *Emotional intelligence.* New York: Bantam.

Gordon, Thomas. 1974. *Teacher effectiveness training.* New York: Peter H. Whyden.

Groff, Linda. 2002. A holistic view of peace education. *Social Alternatives*, 21 (1): 7-10.

Hanh, Thich Nhat. 1996. Being peace. In *Peace is the way*, ed. Walter Wink, 153-158. Maryknoll, NY: Orbis Books.

Hames-García, Michael. 2000. Who are our people? Challenges for a theory of social identity. In *Reclaiming identity*, eds. Paula M.L. Moya and Michael R. Hames-García, 102-129. Berkeley: University of California Press.

Hammack, Philip. 2009. The cultural psychology of American-based coexistence programs for Israeli and Palestinian youth. In *Peace education in conflict and post-conflict societies: comparative perspectives*, eds. Claire McGlynn, Michalinos Zembylas, Zvi Bekerman, and Tony Gallagher. New York: Palgrave Macmillan.

Hanh, Thich Nhat. 1991. *Peace is every step.* New York: Bantam.

———. 1992. *Touching peace: Practicing the art of mindful living.* Berkeley, CA: Parallax.

———. 1996. *Being peace.* Berkeley, CA: Parallax Press.

Hanvey, Robert G. 1982. An attainable global perspective. *Theory Into Practice* XXI (3).

Harding, Vincent. 2000. We must keep going: Martin Luther King, Jr. and the future of America. In *Peace is the Way*, Walter Wink, ed. 193-203. Maryknoll, NY: Orbis Books.

Harris, Ian A. 1999. Types of peace education. In *How children understand war and peace*, eds. Amiram Raviv, Louis Oppenheimer, and Daniel Bar-Tal, 299-310. San Francisco: Jossey-Bass.

Harris, Ian, and Mary Lee Morrison. 2004. *Peace education.* Jefferson, North Carolina: McFarland & Company.

Harris, Ian, and John Synott. 2002. Peace education for a new century, *Social Alternatives,* 21 (1): 3-6.

Hatkoff, Isabella, Craig Hatkoff, and Paula Kahumbu. 2006. *Owen and Mzee: The true story of a remarkable friendship.* New York: Scholastic.

Hawley, Willis, and Gary Sykes. 2007. *The keys to effective schools.* Thousand Oaks, CA: Corwin.

Healing Path, The: A Magazine for Earth, Body, Mind, and Spirit. Fort Collins, CO: BellaSpark Productions. See www.healingpath.org

Henson, Kenneth. 2006. *Curriculum planning.* Long Grove, IL: Waveland.

hooks, bell. 1994. *Teaching to transgress: Education as the practice of freedom.* London: Routledge.

hooks, bell. 2003. *Teaching community: A pedagogy of hope.* New York: Henry Holt.

Howard, Gary R. 2006. *We can't teach what we don't know: White teachers, multiracial school.* New York: Teachers College Press.

Inouye, Harumitsu, Liane Louie-Badua, and Maura Wolf. 2006. Six billion paths to peace: Reflecting on the power of service and leadership to create global harmony. In *Leadership is global: Co-creating a more humane and sustainable world,* eds. Walter Link, Thaís Corral & Mark Gerzon. Boston: Global Leadership Network.

Jensen, Derrick. 2004. *Walking on water.* White River Junction, VT: Chelsea Green.

Jian, Juin-Yin, Ann M. Bisantz, and Colin G. Drury. 2000. Foundations for an empirically determined scale of trust in automated systems. *International Journal of Cognitive Ergonomics,* 4 (1): 53 - 71.

Johnson, David, and Roger Johnson. 1999. *Learning together and alone.* Boston: Allyn and Bacon.

Kandaswamy, Priya. 2007. Beyond colorblindness and multiculturalism. *Radical Teacher,* 80: 6-11.

Karpman, Stephen. n.d. The Drama Triangle. http://www.karpmandramatriangle.com.

Kees, Nathalie. 2003. Creating safe learning environments. In *Teaching diversity: Challenges and complexities, identities and integrity,* eds. William Timpson, Silvia Canetto, Evelinn Borrayo, and Raymond Yang, 55-63. Madison, WI: Atwood Publishing.

Kees, Nathalie, and Patricia Lashwood. 1996. Compassion fatigue and school personnel: Remaining open to the affective needs of students. *Educational HORIZONS,* 75 (1): 41-44.

Kelly, Philip. 2002 *Multiculturalism reconsidered.* Cambridge, UK: Polity Press.

Kenney, Shirley. 1998. *Reinvigorating undergraduate education:* The Boyer Commission on educating undergraduates in the research university. Princeton, NJ: Carnegie Commission.

Kincheloe, Joe L., and Shirley R. Steinberg. 1997. *Changing multiculturalism.* Buckingham: Philadelphia, Open University Press.

King, Coretta. 1984. *The words of Martin Luther King, Jr.* New York: Newmarket Press.

King, Martin Luther, Jr. 2000. Facing the challenge of a new age. In *Peace is the way,* Walter Wink, ed., 178-186. Maryknoll, NY: Orbis Books.

Kliese, Don. 2006. In *Long shadows: Veterans' paths to peace,* ed. David Giffey, 251-262. Madison, WI: Atwood Publishing.

Kneller, Jane. 2003. Recalling the canon. In *Teaching diversity,* eds. William M. Timpson, Silvia Canetto, Evelinn Borrayo, and Ray Yang, eds., 217-226. Madison, WI: Atwood Publishing.

Krathwohl, David R., Benjamin S. Bloom, and Bertran B. Masia. 1964. *Taxonomy of educational objectives: The classification of educational goals, Handbook II: The affective domain.* New York: McKay.

Krishnamurti, Jiddu, and David Bohm. 1986. *The future of humanity: A conversation*. San Francisco: Harper and Row.

Kuhn, Thomas. 1970. *The structure of scientific revolutions*. Chicago: University of Chicago Press.

Larzelere, Robert E., and Ted L. Huston. 1980. The dyadic trust scale: Toward understanding interpersonal trust in close relationships. *Journal of Marriage and the Family*, 42: 595-604.

Lee, John D., and Neville Moray. 1994. Trust, Self-confidence, and Operators' Adaptation to Automation. *International Journal of Human-Computer Studies*, 40 (1): 153-184.

Lin, Jing. 2006. *Love, peace, and wisdom in education: Vision for education in the 21st century*. Lanham, MD: Rowman and Littlefield.

———. 2008. Constructing a global ethic of universal love, forgiveness, and reconciliation: The role of peace education in the twenty-first century. In *Transforming education for peace*, eds. Jing Lin, Edward J. Brantmeier, and Christa Bruhn. Greenwich, CT: Information Age Publishing.

Lin, Jing, Edward J. Brantmeier, and Christa Bruhn, eds. 2008. *Transforming education for peace*. Greenwich, CT: Information Age Publishing.

Little, Judith W. 2007. Professional communication and collaboration. In *The keys to effective schools*, ed. Willis D. Hawley, 51-65. Thousand Oaks, CA: Corwin.

Lowman, Joseph. 2000. *Mastering the Techniques of Teaching*. San Francisco: Jossey-Bass.

Lucero, Rodrick. 2008. *Interactive activities for the classroom*. Seminar for the master teacher initiative of the Institute of Teaching and Learning, Colorado State University. February 19, 2008.

Lynagh, Nichola, and Mary Potter. 2005. Joined-up: developing good relations in the school community. (Available at www.nicie.org/archive/Joined-Up.pdf.) Belfast, Northern Ireland: Northern Ireland Council for Integrated Education and Corrymeela Community.

Macfarlane, Angus, Ted Glynn, Tom Cavanagh, and Sonja Bateman. 2007. Creating culturally safe schools for Maori students. *Australian Journal of Indigenous Education*, 36: 65-76.

Mahalingham, Ram, and Cameron McCarthy. 2000. *Multicultural curriculum: New directions for social theory, practice, and policy*. New York: Routledge.

Mandela, Nelson. 1994. *Long walk to freedom: The autobiography of Nelson Mandela*. Boston: Little Brown.

Maslow, Abraham. 1959. *New knowledge in human values*. New York: Harper & Row.

McGlynn, Claire. 2001. The impact of post primary integrated education in Northern Ireland on past pupils: A study. EdD dissertation, University of Ulster at Jordanstown.

McGlynn, Claire, Ulrike Niens, Ed Cairns, and Miles Hewstone. 2004. Moving out of conflict: the contribution of integrated schools in Northern Ireland to identity, attitudes, forgiveness, and reconciliation. *Journal of Peace Education, 1 (2):* 147-163.

McGlynn, Claire, Michalinos Zembylas, Zvi Bekerman, and Tony Gallagher. 2009. *Peace education in conflict and post-conflict societies: comparative perspectives.* New York: Palgrave Macmillan.

McIntosh, Peggy. 1989. White privilege: Unpacking the invisible knapsack. *Peace and Freedom.* July/August: 10-12.

McKeachie, Wilbert, and Marilla Svinicki. 2006. *Teaching tips: Strategies, research, and theory for college and university teachers.* Boston: Houghton Mifflin.

Middletown, Val. 2003. Reaching the congregation, not just the choir: Conquering resistance to diversity. In *Teaching diversity*, eds. William Timpson, Silvia Canetto, Evelinn Borrayo, and Ray Yang, 103-115. Madison, WI: Atwood Publishing.

Mortenson, Greg, and David Pelin. 2006. *Three cups of tea.* New York: Penguin.

Muir, Bonnie M., and Neville Moray. 1996. Trust in Automation: Part II. Experimental studies of trust and human intervention in a process control simulation. *Ergonomics*, 39 (3): 429-460.

Ndura, Elavie. 2007. Calling institutions of higher education to join the quest for social justice and peace. *Harvard Educational Review*, 77 (3): 345-350.

Nearing, Helen. 1992. *Loving and leaving the good life.* White River Junction, VT: Chelsea Green Publishing Company.

Nearing, Helen, and Scott Nearing. 1970. *Living the good life.* NY: Schocken Books, Inc.

Nieto, Sonia. 2000. *Affirming diversity: The sociopolitical context of multicultural education.* New York: Longman.

Noddings, Nel. 1992. *The challenge to care in schools: An alternative approach to education.* New York: Teachers College Press.

———. 2003. *Happiness and education.* New York: Cambridge University Press.

Nolan, Paul. 2009. From conflict society to learning society: Lessons from the peace process in Northern Ireland. In *Peace education in conflict and post-conflict societies: Comparative perspectives*, eds. Claire McGlynn, Michalinos Zembylas, Zvi Bekerman, and Tony Gallagher. New York: Palgrave Macmillan.

Northern Ireland Council for Integrated education [NICIE].

———. 2008. *ABC: Promoting an anti-bias approach to education in Northern Ireland.* Belfast: NICIE.

Orr, David. 1994. *Earth in mind.* Washington, DC: Island Press.

Palmer, Parker. 1998. *The courage to teach.* San Francisco: Jossey-Bass.

Palms Middle School. 1997. *Council Voices: A Way of Listening.* VHS Tape. Ojai, CA: Ojai Foundation.

Parekh, Bhikhu. 2006. *Rethinking multiculturalism: Cultural diversity and political theory, 2nd ed.* New York: Palgrave Macmillan.

Peace Pilgrim. n.d. Steps toward inner peace. Shelton CT: Friends of Peace Pilgrim, http://www.peacepilgrim.com.

Perry, William. 1999. *Forms of intellectual and ethical development in the college years.* San Francisco: Jossey-Bass.

Pranis, Kay. 2005. *The little book of circle processes: A new/old approach to peacemaking*. Intercourse, PA: Good Books.

Reagon, Bernice Johnson. 1995. "I Remember, I Believe." Washington DC: Songtalk.

Reardon, Betty. 1999. *Peace education: A review and projections* (No. 17). Malmo, Sweden: Malmo University School of Education.

Reich, Robert. 2002. *Bridging liberalism and multiculturalism in American education*. Chicago: The University of Chicago Press.

Roehlkepartain, Eugene, Elanah Naftali, and Laura Musegades. 1989. *Growing up generous*. Herndon, VA: Alban Institute.

Salomon, Gavriel. 2007. Challenging questions facing education in regions of conflict. Keynote address for Education for Peace International Conference, Vancouver, BC.

Salzberg, Sharon. 1995. *Lovingkindness: The revolutionary art of happiness*. Boston: Shambala Classics.

Sarason, Seymour. 1984. *The nature of schools and the problem of change*. Boston: Allyn and Bacon.

Schatz, Mona. 2003. Using dialogue discussion groups when addressing sensitive topics. In *Teaching diversity*, eds. William M. Timpson, Silvia Canetto, Evelinn Borrayo, and Ray Yang, eds., 117-132. Madison, WI: Atwood Publishing.

Sen, Amartya. 2006. *Identity and violence*. New York: Norton.

Senge, Peter, C. Otto Scharmer, Joseph Jaworski, and Betty Sue Flowers. 2005. *Presence: Exploring profound change in people, organizations, and society*. London: Nicholas Brealey Publishing.

Simpson, Elizabeth. 1972. *The classification of educational objectives in the psychomotor domain: The psychomotor domain, Vol. 3*. Washington, DC: Gryphon House.

Skog, Susan. 2004. *Peace in our lifetime: Insights from the world's peacemakers*. Fort Collins, CO: Cliffrose Communications, LLC.

Sleeter, Christine, and Peter McLaren, eds. 1995. *Multicultural education, critical pedagogy and the politics of difference*. New York: State University of New York Press.

Sontag, Deborah, and Lizette Alvarez. 2008. Across America, deadly echoes of foreign battles. *New York Times*, January 13. http://www.nytimes.com/2008/01/13/us/13vets.html.

Takaki, Ron. 1993. *A different mirror*. Boston: Little Brown.

Tannen, Deborah. 1998. *The argument culture*. New York: Ballentine.

Timpson, William, and Fiona Broadbent, eds. 1995. *Action learning: Experiences and promise*. Brisbane, Australia: Tertiary Education Institute, University of Queensland.

Timpson, William M. 1999. *Metateaching and the instructional map*. Madison, WI: Atwood Publishing.

———. 2002. *Teaching and learning peace*. Madison, WI: Atwood Publishing.

Timpson, William M., and Suzanne Bourgogne. 2002. *Teaching and performing: 2nd edition*. Madison, WI: Atwood Publishing.

Timpson, William, Silvia Canetto, Ray Yang, and Evelinn Borrayo, eds. 2003. *Teaching diversity: Challenges and complexities, identities and integrity.* Madison, WI: Atwood Publishing.

Timpson, William, Ray Yang, Evelinn Borrayo, and Silvia Canetto, eds. 2005. *147 practical tips for teaching diversity.* Madison, WI: Atwood Publishing.

Timpson, William M., Brian Dunbar, Gailmarie Kimmel, Brett Bruyere, Peter Newman, and Hillary Mizia. 2006. *147 practical tips for teaching sustainability: Connecting the environment, the economy, and society.* Madison, WI: Atwood Publishing.

Timpson, William, and Sue Doe. 2008. *Concepts and choices for teaching: 2^(nd) edition.* Madison, WI: Atwood Publishing.

Timpson, William M., Norberto Valdez, and David Giffey. Forthcoming. *From battleground to common ground: Stories of conflict, reconciliation, renewal, and place.* Madison, WI: Atwood Publishing.

Tuala-Warren, Leilani. 2002. *A study into the ifoga: Samoa's answer to dispute healing.* Te Ma ta hauariki Institute occasional paper series, no. 4. Hamilton, New Zealand: Te Ma ta hauariki Institute, University of Waikato.

Tutu, Desmond. 1999. *No future without forgiveness.* New York: Doubleday.

———. 2008. Taking the responsibility to protect. *International Herald Tribune,* February 19, 2008.

United Nations. 1948. Universal Declaration of Human Rights. http://www.un.org/en/documents/udhr/index.shtml.

Ury, William. 1999. *The third side.* New York: Penguin.

Von Oech, Roger. 1986. *A kick in the seat of the pants.* New York: Warner.

Whaley, J. David, and Barbara Piazzi-Georgi. 1997. The link between peacekeeping and peacebuilding. *Conflict Management, Peacekeeping, and Peace-building.* Monograph 10 (April).

Wheatley, Margaret. 1999. *Leadership and the new science: Discovering order in a chaotic world.* San Francisco: Berrett-Koehler.

Whitney, Leanne (Producer & Director). 2007. *Return to the Heart: Councils in Schools.* Ojai Foundation (Website: http://www.ojaifoundation.org)

Williams, Will. 2006. In *Long shadows: Veterans' paths to peace,* ed. David Giffey, 67-83. Madison, WI: Atwood Publishing.

Winkelman, Michael. 2003. Complementary therapy for addiction: Drumming out drugs. *American Journal of Public Health,* 93 (4):647-651.

Zimmerman, Jack, and Virginia Coyle. 1996. *The Way of Council.* Las Vegas, NV: Bramble Books.

Author Biographies

William M. Timpson

Dr. William M. Timpson is a professor in the School of Education at Colorado State University and program chair for the doctoral specialization: Educational Leadership, Renewal, and Change. Within that specialization is one elective option for 15 credits of coursework in Peace and Reconciliation Studies. After receiving his bachelor's degree in American History from Harvard University, Bill went on to teach junior and senior high school in the inner city of Cleveland, Ohio, before moving on to complete a doctoral degree in educational psychology at the University of Wisconsin-Madison. While continuing to work with teachers and staff at various levels of schooling, he has written extensively on postsecondary instruction and innovation. Along with numerous articles, chapters, and grants, he has written or co-authored fourteen books including several that address various aspects of teaching diversity, sustainability, peace, and reconciliation. In 2006 he served as a Fulbright Senior Specialist on peace and reconciliation studies at the UNESCO Centre in Northern Ireland. In his work, Timpson draws on extensive experiences abroad including travels to Northern Ireland in 2003 and 2008, Guatemala in 2004, Eastern Europe in 2002, South Africa, Nepal, and India in 2001, and two years of work in Australia (1993-1995). Bill has been an active member of the Peace Education Special Interest Group of the American Educational Research Association.

Edward J. Brantmeier

Dr. Edward J. Brantmeier is an assistant professor in the School of Education at Colorado State University. He serves as Co-Chair of the Interdisciplinary Studies Program in Peace and Reconciliation Studies. Ed earned a bachelor's degree in English with minors in anthropology and English as a second language from the University of Wisconsin-Stevens Point. He earned a master's degree in international and comparative education and a Ph.D. in history, philosophy, and education policy studies from Indiana University-Bloomington. His Ph.D. minors included India studies and anthropology. Ed's current research interests include: peace education, multicultural education, and critical social theory in the context of teacher education and educational leadership. He teaches multicultural education and foundations courses at the undergraduate and graduate levels. He has authored or co-authored articles in the following select journals: Theory and Research in Social Education; Journal of Peace Education; Journal of American Indian Education; International Education; Forum on Public Policy; and Infactis Pax. He serves as a co-editor for a book series on peace education with Information Age Publishing. Ed is currently co-editing a book entitled Spirituality, Religion, and Peace Education. He was recently selected as a Fulbright Scholar in Peace Studies to India. Ed has been an active member of the Peace Education Special Interest Group of the American Educational Research Association.

Nathalie Kees

Dr. Nathalie Kees is an associate professor of counseling and career development in the School of Education at Colorado State University. She has been involved in social justice activities for over 20 years and is currently on the board of the Peace and Reconciliation Studies certificate program at CSU. Her research is in the areas of women's issues in counseling, spirituality and counseling, multicultural education, and effective group facilitation. She served as guest editor for the *Journal for Specialists in Group Work* special issue on women's groups and the *Journal of Counseling and Development* special issue on women's issues in counseling. She founded the Women's Interest Network for the American Counseling Association and has co-authored a book with Dr. Judy Whichard called *Manager as Facilitator.* Dr. Kees also serves on the board of the 2Hearts4Lacy: The Lacy Jo Miller Foundation and is a frequent group trainer for Pathways Hospice.

Tom Cavanagh

Dr. Tom Cavanagh resides in Fort Collins, Colorado, and is on faculty with the Richard W. Riley College of Education and leadership at Walden University. His specialization is as a methodologist. Dr. Cavanagh has degrees from four post-high school institutions, including graduate degrees in Organizational Leadership from Regis University in Denver, and Educational Leadership from Colorado State University in Fort Collins, Colorado. Following graduation with his Ph.D., he spent a year in New Zealand on a Fulbright Fellowship. His research interests focus on the areas of restorative justice and restorative practices in schools; ethnography as the holistic study of organizations and schools as systems; exploring how we can create peaceful and caring relationships; exploring what young people want to learn about (a) peace, (b) legitimating the reality of their lives, which are filled with violence and war, and (c) discovering and encouraging their passion for living together in peace; how schools can use restorative practices to respond to student wrongdoing and conflict in conjunction with a culturally appropriate pedagogy of relations in classrooms, under the umbrella of a culture of care, to create safe schools. Tom has been an active member of the Peace Education Special Interest Group of the American Educational Research Association.

Claire McGlynn

Dr. Claire McGlynn teaches at the School of Education, Queen's University, Belfast, Northern Ireland, where she is course director for the taught doctoral program and co-ordinates an MSc in Diversity and Inclusion. Prior to this she taught extensively in London and Northern Ireland, including initial teacher education at Stranmillis University College, Belfast. She has also been involved in various cross-community initiatives including serving as a founder teacher of New-Bridge Integrated College in County Down (established 1995). Her research interests lie in gaining understanding of the potential of integrated education to rebuild social cohesion in other countries damaged by ethnic conflict, including Israel. Along with Dr. Zvi Bekerman, she edited *Addressing Ethnic Conflict through Peace Education*, a book on sustained international peace education efforts (2007). She also edited *Peace Education in Conflict and Post-Conflict Societies: Comparative Perspectives* (McGlynn, Zembylas, Bekerman, and Gallagher 2009). Claire is a member of the editorial board of the *Journal of Peace Education*, a board member of the Peace Education Commission of the International Peace Research Association and an advisor to the Northern Ireland Council for Integrated Education. She is also a member of an expert panel on teacher education for diversity for the Organisation for Economic Co-operation and Development (OECD) in Europe and the Peace Education Special Interest Group of the American Educational Research Association.

Elavie Ndura-Ouédraogo

Dr. Elavie Ndura-Ouédraogo is an associate professor of education in the Initiatives in Educational Transformation program in George Mason University's College of Education and Human Development. She holds degrees from Burundi, England, and the United States. Her interdisciplinary scholarship focuses on critical multicultural and peace education, and immigrants' acculturation. Along with writing chapters for several books, she edited *Seeds of New Hope: Pan-African Peace Studies for the Twenty-First Century* (Africa World Press 2009) with Matt Meyer. Her scholarly articles have appeared in *Harvard Educational Review; Peace and Change; Journal of Adult and Adolescent Literacy; Language, Culture, and Curriculum; Multicultural Perspectives; Multicultural Education; American Secondary Education; Intercultural Education; Culture of Peace Online Journal; Journal of Peace Education*; and other publications.

She formerly served as board member for the Center for Holocaust, Genocide, and Peace Studies as well as president and founder of the Northern Nevada chapter of the National Association for Multicultural Education. She currently serves on the national board of the Peace and Justice Studies Association and the Peace Education Special Interest Group of the American Educational Research Association. She is the founder and coordinator of the Burundi Schools Project, which collects and distributes donations of instructional materials to benefit schools in Burundi.